Praise for So Who is God, Anyway?:

"Five Stars! Edgy but kind exploration of God's existence and nature...the sense of humor seasons the text like a good dash of salt and pepper. If there's one book on God to read this year, please make it 'So Who is God Anyway?' by G.S. Payne."
—*Reader Views*

"A well-written and convincing rumination on the divine. Payne is especially skilled at introducing difficult concepts with an engaging, often humorous prose style." —*Kirkus Reviews*

"With wit, humanity, and inviting prose, *So Who is God Anyway?* explains complex philosophical concepts clearly and accurately...Payne targets an audience of skeptics, but open-minded people of any religious tradition can find value in his musings." —*BookLife* (Editor's Pick)

"A fascinating exploration. With humor, wit, and thought-provoking insights, Payne makes a convincing case that there is more to God than meets the eye...Whether you're seeking personal growth or a new perspective on life, Payne's work will captivate and challenge you to think beyond what you have been taught." —*Midwest Book Review*

"Filled with humor...Payne's exceptional research is delivered as if he's talking to you at his home while you sip a glass of lemonade. Five stars!" —*Readers' Favorite*

"A thoughtful and accessible approach for the lay believer or nonbeliever who wants a firmer basis in understanding what and how to believe." —*IndieReader*

So Who is God, Anyway?

An (UN)orthodox Theory for
Doubters, Skeptics, and Recovering
Fundamentalists

G. S. Payne

Five Boroughs Media & Publishing

So Who is God, Anyway?
An Unorthodox Theory for Doubters, Skeptics, and Recovering Fundamentalists

G. S. Payne

FIRST EDITION

Manufactured in the United States of America

Paperback ISBN: 979-8-9894749-0-5
Hardcover ISBN: 979-8-9894749-1-2
eBook ISBN: 979-8-9894749-2-9

Library of Congress Control Number: 2023922557

Five Boroughs Media & Publishing
(info@fiveboroughsbooks.com)

Contents

"We got loud guitars and big suspicions,
Great big guns and small ambitions,
And we still argue over who is God."

—Sheryl Crow, "Hard to Make a Stand"

INTRODUCTION

About ten years ago, I was having lunch (a blackened grouper sandwich and a Yuengling draft, as I best recall) with a friend of mine. Even though you're not supposed to discuss religion or politics with people, even friends, we discussed both that day. At one point, "Steve"—not his real name (his real name is Tom)—mentioned that he was fairly sure there's no such thing as God.

"We're pretty much on our own," he declared, swiping a few of my fries.

"That's a pretty bold statement," I said to Steve.

"Yeah, well, it is what it is," he said. This was right around the time when that inane expression had just started popping up. I wasn't sick of it yet, but I was getting there.

"Have you done the research?" I asked.

Steve chortled. "What, you mean, like, read the Bible?"

"No, no," I said. "The *research*."

"Like what?"

"Like the 2,500 years of philosophical thought that's come down to us, starting with the ancient Greeks, and even before them, and on to these very times. There have been a lot of really smart people over the years who have weighed in on the question of God, you know. Even scientists."

As it happened, Steve hadn't done the research. Like most people, Steve never had the time. Or, frankly, the inclination. He'd been busy with, you know, life and stuff. And had he the inclination, where would he have even started? With 2,500 years of information, there's a lot to sift through. Besides, the exercise seemed futile to Steve. "Payne," he said, "I'm sure the really smart people all had very interesting things to say, but if there was any kind of consensus, don't you think we'd know about it? Also, are you going to eat your pickle?"

Steve made a good point. Where *is* the consensus? I had the same concern at one time. Nevertheless, in contrast to Steve, I had the inclination to do the research and see what the big-brained people of history have had to say about the matter, consensus or no consensus. Why? To this day, I don't know. I only know that for as long as I can remember, I've been fascinated by the big questions of life, including the questions of God's existence and God's nature. And so I have always studied—strictly as a hobbyist, mind you—philosophy. I find it a fun pursuit, the way other people find table tennis fun, or stamp collecting, or, say, extreme ironing.[1] I never expected to come to any definitive conclusions.

But a funny thing happened along the way. Gradually, I did come to some definitive conclusions about God. Well, definitive in *my* mind, anyway. Would they be definitive in yours? Maybe. Let's find out. That's what this book is about. The material that follows is the distillation of all the research I have done over the course of about thirty years. So to answer the question of where one would

---

1. Believe it or not, this is actually a thing. Extreme ironing (EI) enthusiasts go to remote and dangerous locations, set up ironing boards, and... iron. (I swear, I am *not* making this up.)

even start, I might humbly suggest right here, with the book you hold in your hands.

But be advised. The conclusions I have reached about God are probably not what you are expecting. Within the pages of this book, I am going to describe a concept of God that is not often talked about and may even be a concept you have never heard of.[2] But I will lay this concept out in a logical, rational way, using as my only weapons, and with nothing up my sleeve, the tools of the philosopher, which is to say, a line of reasoning that I hope will make for a solid, cogent, compelling case. (And hopefully a fun little trip to boot.)

This is not, in other words, a testimony. I have nothing against the many books recounting the lives of people who had reached the bottom of life's ladder and were wallowing in the gutter, only to discover the miracle of Jesus or God or Allah, and who then turned their lives around when they had completely run out of hope. These can be beautiful stories, and I suppose the world can always take one more of them. I just don't have such a story, and it has always sort of stuck in my craw (wherever the craw is) that so few people have presented an idea of God simply on its own merits, without having to refer to a lived or witnessed miracle as evidence. Not everyone witnesses miracles, after all, including me. Can God be accessible to us too? I believe so. As this book will suggest, God can be more than accessible.

The order of this book represents, roughly, my own philosophical journey, starting out with the question of whether God exists in the first place, followed by a discussion on the nature of a god

---

2. You'll notice that nowhere in this book will I claim to describe God, an impossible task. Rather, I will describe a *concept* of God. (And sometimes I will describe what I believe God isn't.)

that would exist, and finishing with what I believe to be a startling revelation about religion—namely, that *all* the world's major religions recognize the concept of God that I argue for but that few of these religions, in their mainstream iterations, have advanced this particular concept through doctrine or tradition.

Importantly—and I cannot emphasize this enough—there is nothing in this book that is new. There's not a single concept that has come from the imagination of yours truly. I am a philosopher–hobbyist and a researcher. I am not a philosopher, theologian, or scientist. The information contained in this book comes from some of the biggest-brained folks to have ever lived on this planet. These ideas are not mine. They belong to the smartest people I could find, and I have brought them all together in one place just so you can see what *they* have to say about the big questions. If you don't like what you read, take it up with them. I'm just the messenger.

Moreover, in the interests of accuracy and validity, I've spent a lot of effort making sure the book you are about to read passes philosophical muster. To that end, I want to thank Dr. Loriliai Biernacki of the University of Colorado, Dr. Matthew Benton of Seattle Pacific University, and Dr. Perry Hendricks of the University of Minnesota, Morris—all real, live, bona fide, professional *philosophers*, and all very encouraging, very willing to review my work, and kind enough to point out the flaws and weak spots in my thinking.[3] This doesn't necessarily mean that they agree with everything you read here, but I have come to understand that dis-

---

3. There are branches of philosophy, as you might imagine. This illustrious group represents the specialties of philosophy of religion, epistemology, logic, and ethics, with interests in science, language, and the philosophy of mind. Smart people. (And all really nice!)

agreement is why philosophy exists in the first place. (Philosophy, it turns out, is a good field to get into if you like arguing with people.) The point is, I have not gone about this on my own; I have relied on some extraordinarily smart people to help me get things right.

It's important, however, for us to not allow ourselves to be intimidated by the big thinkers of history and academia. I don't know about you, but I happen to think the questions about God are too important to be left exclusively in the hands of the philosophers and theologians and other big-brained folks, with their near-inscrutable writings and esoteric terminologies. Why should they have all the fun? In this book, we're going to explore the matter of God, you and I, using the knowledge of the smart guys, but the language of real people. You want to make sense of it, too, don't you? Don't you deserve to be a part of the conversation? Shouldn't you be invited to the party? With this book, we're going to crash the joint.

In the end, my hope is that what you read here will at least kindle some kind of curiosity in you. Maybe you'll want to learn more about what is presented here. You must have been a little curious to begin with; otherwise, why would you have picked up this book? Perhaps you're a skeptic or a doubter (hence the subtitle), but maybe there's a small piece of you that wonders if, damn it, maybe there really *is* a God. Or maybe you're an ex-fundamentalist. You've really only ever been presented with one concept of God, you've ultimately found it dissatisfying, and you're wondering if there's another way to look at the whole God thing.

No matter your motivation, it is what it is, and I'm glad you're here. You may disagree with every conclusion I draw from the smart people I have assembled, but I *absolutely guarantee*[4] that by the end of this book, you will at least have learned something valuable (meaning something impressive that you can repeat at a cocktail party).

A final note: I have made the material herein as understandable as possible, but if at any time you have a question about what something means, feel free to raise your hand and call out. No, wait. That won't work. Instead, please refer to the glossary in the back of the book, which I have included *just for you.* (Because that's the kind of guy I am.)

Without any further ado, I say we get started on this little journey of ours, a journey that I hereby dedicate to all the Steves of the world (real name: Tom). It was that lunch, after all, that put the idea of this book into my head. As you can see, I finally got around to writing it. And, yes, you can have my pickle.

---

4. Not an actual guarantee. —*Publisher*

Chapter One

What Can Be Known

This book puts forth a theory. (You can tell because it says so right on the cover.) But here's the thing about theories: they have to be backed up with something. A person can't just run around throwing theories about without any kind of evidentiary support. Actually, I take that back: in these modern internet days, that happens all the time. Sometimes, the theories become full-blown conspiracies, fed by nothing more than social media and the power of repetition. Maybe even a clever meme. But we're looking for something stronger than that here, aren't we? Sure we are. You're doubting the existence of God. You're the inquisitive type, however, so you're willing to listen to an argument for God's existence—but it had better be a damn good one. You didn't spend good money on this book[1] just to have your time wasted. There are plenty of other books for that. You want proof. You want evidence. "C'mon, Payne," you're saying. "Show me the goods!"

The question, of course, becomes this: What exactly would constitute evidence? What would be sufficient to sway you toward a worldview that would include some conception of God? And what would that conception be? That's the real key, right? If you doubt God's existence, I'm willing to bet it's because you're not

---

1. Thanks, by the way!

1

satisfied with any conception of God you've been presented with. God doesn't make sense to you. If you're like me, the traditional image of the bearded old man sitting on his throne in the sky, watching and judging us, just doesn't cut the mustard. I mean, we're not five years old, right? If you're a recovering fundamentalist, I'll bet the doubt about this particular conception—the one we're pretty much all introduced to as children—especially resonates. It might be the primary reason you left fundamentalism behind. Or maybe you just got tired of the dogmatism. But, unwilling to throw out the proverbial baby with the bathwater, you're wondering if there's another way. Whatever your motivations for reading this book, let us—you and me together—see if we can arrive at some sort of sensical, maybe even satisfying, conception of God. (Possibly even one without all the dogma.) I'll present some ideas, and we'll see where they lead.

But first things first. The conception question will have to wait for now because the *nature* of God is a different question from that of the *existence* of God. Let's not get too far ahead of ourselves. No concept of God's nature is going to prove satisfactory if you don't believe in God's existence. So, let's talk about the reality of there being a god. Let's talk about evidence. Let's talk about *knowing*. What do these words even mean? Are there objective proofs? Can I offer evidence that would make everyone who ever reads this book believe 100 percent that God exists? Of course not. I can't even offer a universally agreed-to proof that the Earth is round. Somebody, somewhere, would doubt me. In fact, there's an entire society of people called "Flat-Earthers" who think this whole "round" thing is a myth.[2] The problem is that no matter the question, we all come at it from our own individual perspec-

---

2. I shit you not. Look 'em up.

tives. We each come from different backgrounds. Different sets of parents. Different childhoods. Different places, social influences, and educations. And these individual perspectives can be a problem when it comes to finding agreement on *anything*, much less something as seemingly elusive as the existence of God.

And yet, this problem needn't be a deal-killer.

Let us look closer at this thing called "knowing." Conveniently, there's an entire branch of philosophy, *epistemology*, that deals with the subject of knowledge. The first thing you need to know is that epistemology is *boring*. There. I said it. My apologies to all of you epistemologists out there, but you have to admit that the subject is a dry one. Drier than economics, even, and that's pretty dry. Nevertheless, if we're going to approach this idea of theorizing about the existence of God, we need to acquaint ourselves with some of the concepts that the extraordinarily dry field of epistemology has given us.[3] And we need to do so because, it seems to me, we need to put down some ground rules as to what constitutes proof and evidence and knowledge and what you can realistically expect from a book such as this one. That's only fair to you, right? And I'm nothing if not fair.

Most epistemological discussions actually start out pretty interestingly. Two of the most basic epistemological questions are full of intrigue: 1) What do we know? and 2) How do we know we know it? The problem comes with the answers. You see, there's really no universal agreement here. Epistemologists generally recognize that there are two fundamental types of knowledge (although even this is often in dispute): *propositional* knowledge that something is true and *non-propositional* knowledge *of* something.

---

3. How dry is it? Epistemologists never get invited to parties. I mean never. Think about it. Have you ever met an epistemologist at a party?

The first just means that I know, for example, that two plus two equals four. It's knowledge of facts. All trees are plants. The sun is really hot. The IRS gets pissed if you don't file your taxes. These are simple propositions, and we know them. The second type of knowledge is more like a direct awareness or intuitive kind of thing. I know it's going to rain because I feel it in my bones. I know that if I spill my beer, it's going to make the floor sticky. Non-propositional knowledge often comes to us through experience, through familiarity with something.

Well, right away, we have to discount non-propositional knowledge as a means by which to prove God's existence, right? My experience with God isn't going to do you any good at all. You don't even know me. Why should you believe me if I say I have "experienced" something of God? I should say, however, that we might not want to *totally* discount the significance of religious experience. A recent Pew Research poll reveals that nearly 50 percent of Americans claim to have had "mystical" or "religious" experiences. That seems like it ought to mean something. That's somewhere around 165 million people. Are they all just batshit crazy? Nevertheless, you're looking for something more tangible, aren't you? Yeah, I figured as much. Okay, for the moment, then, we'll stick to propositional knowledge, but I reserve the right to reexamine direct awareness through religious experience later.

Now, propositional knowledge comes in a couple of flavors: empirical and non-empirical (or rational). Empirical knowledge is the kind of knowledge you gain through observation or experimentation. Non-empirical is good old-fashioned reason—something you don't need to see to know. If I told you I was writing this book while taking a Caribbean cruise, you'd figure I was on some type of ship. You don't need to see me on the ship to assume that. You can just use reason. Later on, we'll discover that there are arguments for

God's existence that make use of both types of propositional arguments: rational arguments premised on empirical observations.

Each type of propositional knowledge seems to have its place, but it turns out that there have been some extremely dull arguments over the years between empiricists and rationalists. I'll do you a favor and not recount those arguments here. If you want to do a little deeper dive into what the great minds have had to say about the subject of propositional knowledge over the centuries, I would recommend acquainting yourself with John Locke (1632–1704), George Berkeley (1685–1753), and David Hume (1711–1776) on the side of the empiricists and René Descartes (1596–1650), Gottfried Wilhelm Leibniz (1646–1716), and Baruch Spinoza (1632–1677) on the side of the rationalists. These were some pretty smart guys. How smart? Leibniz wrote his theories in six different languages, and aside from his forays into philosophy, he was fairly adept at math. In fact, he developed calculus. Locke had side interests, too, notably an interest in political theory, and so influenced by Locke was a young American by the name of Thomas Jefferson that you can find his fingerprints all over the Declaration of Independence.

Most philosophers recognize the usefulness of both types of propositional knowledge, but it must be said that so far as the existence of God is concerned, we're really not going to get very far using a purely empirical argument, which is to say an argument based solely on observation or some sort of scientific experiment. After all, if God could be proved scientifically, shouldn't someone have done so by now? Where's the *New York Times* headline that proclaims: "Scientists Prove God's Existence in Shocking Laboratory Experiment"?[4] Now, this is not to say that science hasn't empirically revealed some pretty intriguing things that might make you scratch your head. We'll discuss quantum physics a little later, for instance. The fact is that even scientists, steeped as they are in the ways and means of empiricism, cannot agree on the existence of God. Interestingly, more scientists than you probably imagine are believers. Another Pew Research report reveals that just over half (51 percent!) of American scientists surveyed believe "in God or a higher power." Still, that leaves almost half that do not.

Okay, so direct awareness won't help us, and where propositional knowledge is concerned, neither will empiricism alone. Where does that leave us? Well, it leaves us relying on the *tools of the philosopher*, that's where. We have to rely on *argument*. A line of reasoning. Maybe it's based on observation, or maybe it's based on even more reasoning, but what we're talking about here are arguments produced on rational, logical grounds satisfactorily defended from criticism. This is what philosophers do. A good philosophical argument makes you go, "Cripes, I hate to say it, but I think he's got something there." A good philosophical argument makes you say, "You know, I never really thought of that before" or "I never looked at it that way."

Now, at this point, I know what you're thinking. You're thinking, "'I never looked at it that way?!' That's your test for a good argument? Isn't there something more quantifiable that we can use? Tell me, Payne, what do the *epistemologists* have to say about what makes a good philosophical argument?" Great question. As

---

4. "Damndest thing," Professor Newton Greenblatt told reporters. "We were just kind of fooling around late one night, running computer simulations for the Department of Defense that I can't really talk about, and He just popped up. The Big Kahuna himself! Right there in the lab!" Greenblatt added, "Man, if this doesn't get me a Nobel, what will?"

it happens, the classical view in the field of epistemology, coming down to us from no less of a pillar of philosophy than Plato,[5] is that propositional knowledge can be defined as *justified true belief*.

What the heck does this mean? Well, if something is known, you *believe* it, right? It wouldn't make sense to say that while you don't believe you had eggs for breakfast, you know you did. So, belief has to be a component of knowledge. And, of course, the belief also has to be *true*. Ah, but what is truth? Well, you're not the first person to ask. Pontius Pilate actually put this question to Jesus at his trial, at least according to the Bible. Unfortunately, Jesus didn't answer, but Pilate probably meant it rhetorically, anyway. The question followed Jesus's statement that he'd come into the world to "bear witness unto the truth," and Pilate's question was probably just a way to blow him off and keep the trial moving along.

There are different ideas of what truth is, as you might imagine. There's *the correspondence theory of truth*, which basically states that something is true if it corresponds to how the world is. There's *the coherence theory of truth*, which states that something is true if it falls in line with a bunch of other known things. And then there's *the pragmatic theory of truth*, which values the truth of something by its degree of usefulness.

See? I told you that epistemology was boring.

Okay, look, don't get too hung up on the truth thing. You know what I would use if I were you? I'd use what I'll call *the pornography theory of truth*, borrowing a line from United States Supreme Court justice Potter Stewart, who in 1964 famously said

---

5. And I mean pillar. Twentieth-century philosopher A. N. Whitehead, whom we'll be visiting later, declared that "All of Western philosophy is but a footnote to Plato."

that he couldn't define pornography, but he knew it when he saw it. You could probably also call this "the common-sense theory of truth," but "the pornography theory" has a better ring to it, don't you think? Anyway, use your best judgment to determine if something is true based on what *you* consider satisfactory reasons. There. Good enough. (For now.)

Okay, so something is true, and you believe it. To be *knowledge*, however, it needs one more factor, at least according to Plato. You need to be *justified* in believing it. There are a lot of really tedious arguments about what constitutes justification, but its inclusion as a factor of knowledge is pretty much agreed upon by everyone. An example might help. Let's say I'm walking down the street toward my friend Sweeney's three-story brownstone. My plan is to pop in and see if he wants to go have lunch. I believe he's home. He's always home because, well, where's Sweeney going to go? I'm his only friend, and he's a recluse who never goes anywhere. And so, the truth of his being home is very clear in my mind, comporting as it does with everything I know about Sweeney. But, of course, until I get there, I really don't have sufficient justification to believe that my thoughts on Sweeney's whereabouts are anything I can classify as knowledge. I don't *know* that Sweeney is home. And I won't know until I can justify my belief by, say, seeing him through his bay window as I approach the house. In fact, there he is now. I can see the back of his bald head. He's sitting at his desk, no doubt doing the daily Wordle, as is his custom. I now have knowledge that Sweeney is home.

Using this standard, then, we can say that the existence of God, to be classified as knowledge—meaning that it becomes something you come to *know*—needs to be something you are *justified* in believing to be true. Phew. Glad we got that straightened out.

But wait. As it happens, another smart guy, by the name of Edmund Gettier (1927–2021), came along and discovered a problem with Plato's justified true belief idea.[6] It turns out that you can have a belief that's true and justified, but the belief might not actually be knowledge. Here's how that can happen: I get to Sweeney's front door and let myself in, only to discover that the person at Sweeney's desk is not Sweeney but his twin brother, who isn't doing the Wordle at all. He's doing the crossword puzzle and is currently agonizing over a clue that is asking for an eight-letter word for "stubborn." But here's the thing: Sweeney *is* home. He's upstairs, which I discover when he comes down into the parlor and helps his brother out by offering "obdurate."

It was true that Sweeney was home. Further, since he's always home at that time, I was justified in believing that he was home. That belief was even more justified when I saw what I thought was the back of Sweeney's head. All Plato's conditions were met. And yet, I still didn't have *knowledge*. I only thought I did.

Now, there have been a lot of attempts to answer Gettier. Some philosophers suggest that a fourth condition is necessary, but nobody can seem to agree on what that condition should be. Others think that justified true belief is sufficient but that, in examples like mine, the justification is simply too weak. Even though I had good reason to believe Sweeney was home and indeed saw the back of a head that looked just like Sweeney's, I needed more evidence. The problem with this approach is that it seems to suggest that I damn near need to *see* Sweeney *in* his home (maybe even ask for some ID) before I'm justified in believing he's at home. But then, what's the difference between justification and knowledge? If I saw him in his

---

6. There's always one in the crowd, huh? The proverbial turd in the punchbowl.

home, I wouldn't need to worry about whether I had justified true belief that I could rightly consider *knowledge* of his whereabouts.

Or, to put it in terms relevant to this book, if I could *see* God, I wouldn't need to wonder if my belief in God was justified and true. I wouldn't need epistemology!

So. Where does that lead us? Short of seeing God and experiencing our own direct awareness, which we've agreed is not sufficiently transmissible to others, is it just flat impossible to *know* that God exists, no matter how good an argument someone makes?

For one answer to that question, I'd like to introduce you to the Skeptics. Jim and Marge Skeptic of Muncie, Indiana. Jim's a forklift salesman, and Marge is a hairdresser. They're nice people, the kind of people who would never think of getting in the express lane at the grocery store with more than ten items. The kind of people who would lend you their snowblower if you asked nicely. Hell, Jim would come over and snow-blow your walk and driveway for you. That's the kind of guy he is. And Marge would bring you chicken soup if you weren't feeling well. Homemade.

But the thing about Jim and Marge is this: like a lot of skeptics, they don't believe anybody can know *anything*. Now, we're not necessarily talking about skepticism with respect to God (although it is also that); we're talking about *skepticism* with respect to knowledge in general. Knowledge skeptics believe that nothing can be known. Basically, they like to ask this question: How can we figure out *what* we know without figuring out *how* we know? And then, before you can even answer, they fire this follow-up question at you: How can we figure out *how* we know without figuring out *what* we know?

You see the problem? It's a godawful circle is what it is. In the philosophy world, this is known as "the problem of criterion," and it's even more fundamental than the Gettier problem. David

Hume, one of the aforementioned empiricists, was one of the most famous skeptics, especially when it came to inductive reasoning. When you induce, or infer, a general conclusion from a specific observation or observations, you are engaged in inductive reasoning. Suppose, for example, that I look out the window and see that it's raining. This is no less than a tragedy because I had planned on making a gin and tonic and sitting out by the pool. But at least I know that the rain will eventually stop. How do I know this? Because it always stops. Always. Now, Hume would tell you[7] that you cannot legitimately claim to know that the rain will stop. It might never stop. Or, as my broker is fond of telling me whenever the stock market goes to shit, "Past performance is not a guarantee of future results." Believing that the rain will stop is nothing more than an assumption. An educated one, based on experience, but an assumption just the same.

Of course, strictly speaking, Hume is right. I cannot know something based only on prior experience. And the history of philosophy is full of knowledge skeptics, going all the way back to the ancient Greeks and stretching forward to the present day with Jim and Marge of Muncie, Indiana.

But history is also full of philosophers who have felt that skepticism is a bridge too far. First, skepticism suffers from an inherent contradiction, which you might have already figured out: namely, how can we *know* that nothing can be known? If you're going to be a skeptic, if you're going to go all in on the idea that knowledge is unavailable, then you have to admit that you don't even know *that*. And there's another problem with skepticism: our existence appears to refute it. We seem to know things, and the things we

---

7. With his heavy Scottish brogue that you probably wouldn't be able to understand.

know keep us alive. We know that we need to eat, and we know how to eat. We know what to eat and what not to eat.[8] We know that we need to stay warm in the winter and cool in the summer. We know when we need sleep. Face it: we know *a lot*.

What's needed, really, in this discussion of what we can know, is something useful. Something that can help us. Something that resonates. Bertrand Russell (1872–1970) (a famous agnostic, incidentally) put it like this: "Skepticism, while logically impeccable, is psychologically impossible."

We *need* to believe that we know things, right? Life is absurd otherwise. Maybe even unlivable.

Perhaps what we need is some common sense. And if you think that doesn't sound very philosophical, allow me to introduce you to a philosopher by the name of George Edward Moore (1873–1958). In 1925, Moore wrote a famous essay (well, famous amongst philosopher types) entitled, of all things, "A Defence of Common Sense." Moore talks about things that we know, like how we know our bodies exist and how we know they existed yesterday. In fact, Moore argues that damn it, it's just more reasonable to believe in claims of common sense than it is to believe in skepticism. It's more reasonable, in other words, to believe we can know things than to believe we can't.

Now, this reasonableness standard is interesting, and it seems to me that maybe we can make use of it, even with controversial claims. Listen, I'm willing to make a partial concession to skepticism and acknowledge that we cannot know anything *for absolute certain*. We can't know anything 100 percent. Even the idea that

---

8. We especially know not to order the seafood "special" in a certain restaurant at the San Antonio airport that will remain nameless here. Boy, do we know that.

the Earth is round. Let's give that a 99.9 percent certainty factor. But that's still pretty high. The answers to other questions might be less certain. Maybe 60 percent on the certainty scale. Maybe 30 percent. Maybe 10 percent. At the beginning of this chapter, I said that no matter the question, we all come at it from our own individual perspectives. Consequently, the percentages will vary depending on the person.

At the beginning of this chapter, I also talked about evidence and proof. I wondered (rhetorically) if I could offer evidence that would make everyone who ever reads this book 100 percent believe that God exists. Of course, the answer is no. But do we need 100 percent certainty to believe in God? Would you be willing to believe if you were 90 percent certain? Sixty percent?

Fifty-one percent?

God's existence cannot be definitively proven. However, I believe we can take a page out of George Edward Moore's essay and agree, you and I, on a standard to meet. That standard is this: *it's more reasonable to believe that God exists than to not believe.*

Naturally, defining reasonableness is tricky because it's so subjective. I cannot define it for you. Only you know what "reasonable" means to you. And your definition might be wildly different from your neighbor's. Here's what's interesting: you'd both be right. And you'd both be right because the standard ends up being a personal one because of all the problems with knowledge we discussed above. Any way you slice it, objective knowledge is a bitch.

I suggest we do this: let's examine the proposition "God exists" with an open mind, even if we know going in that we cannot hope to achieve 100 percent certainty. Hey, after all, skepticism informs us that the proposition "God *doesn't* exist" ain't exactly a slam-dunk, either. The proverbial knife cuts both ways. That said, I'm willing to grant that the burden of proof is on the first proposition. Why? Because I am declaring it to you. You were perfectly fine the way things were. Then you spotted this book and said to yourself, "Okay, let's see what this Payne fellow has to say." So, here we are.

Fortunately, you don't have to listen only to me. In this chapter, you've already been introduced to some of the biggest-brained folks in history. You're going to meet a lot more as this journey continues, and I would like to reiterate what I said in the Introduction (which I hope you took the time to read because I think it's really pretty good): there's not a single idea within the pages of this book that is mine. Think of me not as your teacher but as your guide.[9]

And when it's all said and done, at the end of the day, in the final analysis, when the smoke has cleared, when all the clichés have been written, you'll be able to employ your own personal standard of reasonableness to adjudge whether I have presented something that will make you second-guess your own skepticism and doubt or whether instead I'm just completely full of crap. Fair enough? Either way, no hard feelings, okay? You seem like a good person, and I'd still like to be friends with you. Maybe.

---

9. Tips not mandatory but always appreciated.

Chapter Two

The Big 10: Part I

In the last chapter, we determined that we cannot prove God by experience (direct awareness) or science (a form of empiricism). The former is personal knowledge that we cannot rightly transmit to another person, and if such proof as the latter exists, it certainly should have been presented by someone, somewhere, by now.

This leaves us with the tools of the philosopher—the development of arguments for God's existence that are so good that we would be justified in believing their conclusions. But we also learned that justification is a tricky thing, and we are probably right to carry with us (in all matters of propositional knowledge) some degree of skepticism. But not all-out skepticism. Not uber-skepticism. I mean, after all, we accept that we know *some* things, right?

And so we have decided that perhaps common sense should prevail and that ultimately our goal should be to entertain an argument, or arguments, that make it *more* reasonable to believe in God's existence than to *not* believe, with "reasonableness" left as a standard to be defined by the reader. That's you.

History, it turns out, reveals many arguments for the existence of God, some better than others. History also reveals many arguments against the existence of God. Keep in mind that we're not necessarily concerned with arguments for or against any specific concept of God at this point but rather arguments for or against the idea of God in general.

I propose that we cover the pro arguments first, since you're a doubter anyway and probably don't need a rundown of the con arguments, at least at this point. Heck, you've probably got your own. Eventually, though, assuming we make some progress on the pro side, we're going to need to tackle the con arguments. You're going to say, "Oh yeah? Well, what about..." and then you'll launch into some objection or another. You're not going to go down without a fight. Not you. That's just not the way you roll, thank you very much.

But that will all come later. Right now, let's explore the reasoning of some of philosophy's great minds in favor of our proposition. In no particular order, here's a laundry list of arguments that have been presented over the centuries for the proposition that God does, indeed, exist:

- The ontological argument

- The cosmological argument

- The teleological argument

- The historical record

- The moral argument

- The existential argument

- Pascal's wager

- The prevalence of religious experience

- Mind–body dualism

- The aesthetic argument

Now, this list doesn't represent every argument that's ever been made—just some of the more famous and best articulated ones. I'm going to call it the "Big Ten" and hope that the college athletic conference of the same name doesn't sue me. If, as we go along, you decide that you like one, you're welcome to ring the bell, and I'll happily pull the bus over and let you get off. My job will have been done. But I've got a hunch that you're not going to be that easy to please.

The plan is this: We'll spend this chapter and the next three outlining these arguments and touching on their strengths and weaknesses. Then, we'll summarize and put them all together into a more cohesive whole before moving on to the arguments against God's existence to see how that cohesive whole sticks together, if it even does. Maybe it'll be blown apart. We'll just have to see, won't we?

Let's start with *the ontological argument for God*. It's the first on the list, so why not? Ontology is a branch of metaphysics, so we probably ought to define metaphysics first. *Meta* roughly means "after" or "beyond." So we can think of metaphysics as referring to that which is beyond physics. Beyond, in other words, what meets the eye. In fact, metaphysics is the branch of philosophy that we'll be studying pretty much from here on out. Think of this whole discussion as a discussion of metaphysics.

Specifically, ontology deals with the concept of being or existence. Ontology asks, What exists? The question of God's existence is an ontological one, and the ontological argument runs like this: suppose we mean by the idea of "God" the being (if any there is) than which none greater can be conceived. If you don't believe in the actual existence of God, then you believe that such a being exists only in our minds. But wait: this can't be an accurate conception of God because we can still conceive of a *greater* being, right? A greater being would be one that exists in reality. Therefore, the being than which none greater can be conceived must exist. In reality. See?

Boom. Mic drop.

Hmm... I don't hear you ringing the bell.

You're probably right to hold off. The ontological argument was first proposed in 1078 by Saint Anselm of Canterbury (1033/4–1109) in a meditation titled the *Proslogion*, but others have argued similarly, including Descartes in the seventeenth century and Leibniz in the eighteenth century. Even in the twentieth century, variations of the ontological argument were put forth by such well-respected thinkers as famed mathematician Kurt Gödel and American philosophers Norman Malcolm and Alvin Plantinga.

The variations are interesting but, I fear, not especially effective at advancing the original proposition, at least as far as I'm concerned. Criticisms of Saint Anselm's argument came almost immediately. A Benedictine monk in France (a believer, no less) by the name of Gaunilo asked why you couldn't use the same logic to prove the existence of anything. He proposed using a mythical island. If one can conceive of the greatest and most perfect island, then that island must exist; otherwise, it wouldn't be the greatest and most perfect island. *In your face, Anselm*, he seemed to be saying.[1] Anselm replied that he was talking about *beings*, not islands. Still, it seems as if Gaunilo has a point.

Hume, empiricist that he was, responded to Anselm as well, essentially asking why anything necessarily *has* to exist. Empirical data, after all, can tell us only what exists and not what doesn't. Philosophical giant Immanuel Kant[2] (1724–1804) objected to the premise. Why, he asked, does greatness necessarily require existence? Can't something be great without existing? What does existing really add? In fact, Kant didn't even regard existence as a property, arguing essentially that existence isn't a characteristic of something in the way that, say, height is a characteristic.

Personally, I find the argument kind of fun but not convincing. To me, it seems more like wordplay, and it just doesn't *feel* right. Bertrand Russell once put it like this: "It is easier to feel convinced that the [ontological] argument must be fallacious than it is to find out precisely where the fallacy lies." On the whole, I think I agree with Kant. But that's me. (And Kant.) As with any of these arguments, if you find something that resonates in some way with you, feel free to put this book down and do a little research on your own. I'll wait right here. But in the meantime, I think maybe we should move on to more promising arguments.

Now, *the cosmological argument* has potential. This is one of the most cherished arguments, and if the question of God's existence were a popularity contest, it would definitely be in the running. In fact, it would probably win. It would be hoisted onto our shoulders and paraded around with Queen's "We Are the Champions"

---

1. Actually, people were much more polite back then, especially these two guys who had great respect for each other. Thank God Twitter didn't exist then, am I right? (Or whatever it's called now.)

2. Well, "giant" in a metaphorical sense. Kant was all of five feet, two inches.

blaring through the streets. Alas, the question of God's existence is not a popularity contest. Crowd-pleasing does not equal truth.[3]

But here's what makes the cosmological argument so appealing. It points out that everything we know in the physical world seems to have a cause. Nothing just pops up out of nowhere. And if you extend this line of thinking backward in time, it stands to reason that there must have been a very *first* cause. Of everything! This provides a convenient explanation for nothing less than existence. After all, perhaps the most fundamental philosophical question of all time is this: Why is there something rather than nothing? The cosmological argument gives us an answer.

If God didn't create the universe, then how did it come to be? How can something pop up out of nothing? How can something be caused without a cause? Think about it: in nothingness, not even potentialities exist. When I say nothingness, by the way, I mean *nothing*ness. I'm not talking about a bunch of empty space. I'm talking about a state where even space doesn't exist. Where time doesn't exist. Where existence itself doesn't exist. Nothing. Nada. Zilch. Without a creator (God) to cause space and time to come into existence, how did space and time do so? How did the universe come to be? There is no other explanation: therefore, God.

That's the cosmological argument in its essence. We can credit Saint Thomas Aquinas (1225–1274) with articulating and pop-

---

3. Today's political demagoguery notwithstanding.

ularizing the cosmological argument in his *Summa Theologica*,[4] but the idea of causation goes back to the ancient Greeks. Aristotle advanced the concept of a "prime mover." And centuries before Aquinas, Arab philosopher Ibn Sina (980–1037) developed what's known today as "the argument from contingency," a variation of the cosmological argument that puts forth the idea that everything is contingent, meaning that all things are dependent on something else. But then there must be something non-contingent, or necessary, on which the set of all contingent things depends. And this necessary thing must be God. (This answers the question, in case you were thinking of asking it, of what created God. Necessary entities don't need creators. Only contingent entities do.[5]) Any way you put it, you can see why the idea of a first cause is so popular. It's got a logic to it that seems, at first blush, irrefutable. Something cannot come out of nothing. A creator is necessary, and that proves God.

But the argument is not invincible. First, the cosmological argument assumes a starting point. But what if there wasn't one? What if there wasn't a point of creation? What if the universe has been in existence since... forever? There needn't be a cause if time past is infinite because there was no moment of conception that required a cause.

---

4. *Summa Theologica* ("Summary of Theology") is a massive work that, interestingly, you can buy on Amazon. I'm serious. (Not the original, of course.) It's several volumes in length. Over 5000 pages! Aquinas was still writing it when he died, so it remains unfinished, making one wonder how long the final draft of this "summary" would have been.

5. A more recent defense for a necessary being, using twentieth-century advances in modal logic, can be found in *Necessary Existence* (Oxford University Press, 2018) by Alexander R. Pruss and Joshua L. Rasmussen. (If you're looking for a good read. I mean, after this one.)

Theists have an answer to that. Medieval Muslim philosophers first proposed the idea that if the past is infinite, then we could never have arrived at our point in time. Think of a line of dominoes falling over one by one, and the line is running right past you. You look to your left where the line of falling dominoes is coming from, expecting that the one directly in front of you will soon be struck. Ah, but if the line to your left goes on infinitely, without an initial domino, then how will the line of fallings ever reach you? They won't. You'll be waiting forever, like a man waiting for his car at a valet stand, where it turned out that the attendant he gave his keys to didn't even really work at the stand. He just put on a red vest and made the man *think* he was a valet attendant, driving off with the man's car and eventually ditching it, never to be found again. Yeah. You'll be like that guy.

But that's not an invincible argument, either. You could argue (and many have) that time is merely a construct of the human brain. Maybe we *perceive* a specific direction of time in order to make sense of life here in the universe, a place where, for all we know, time is actually circular. Or maybe everything happens all at once. There's no need for a starting point because time does not proceed linearly the way we think that it does.

Well, sure, maybe. We'll be addressing some of this time stuff later on, but even with the more commonly believed unidirectionality of time, it has to be admitted that theists still have a problem with the idea of a causative agent. Here's the thing about causation: it's a temporal activity. It requires... time. What sense does it make that the universe was caused when time didn't exist at the moment (an increment of time!) of causation? Wouldn't it make more sense to believe that the universe has always existed? Well, except for that domino thing. But Payne, you remind me, most physicists and cosmologists (and cosmetologists, for all we know) believe in the Big Bang theory of the universe's origin, and the Big Bang theory recognizes that at the precise point when the universe began—referred to as the "singularity"—all physical laws, as we know them, broke down.

And with that, you think you're off the hook. An explanation for the beginning of the universe isn't required because, well, the moment was nonsensical anyway.

I dunno. You have to admit that sounds kind of weak. At this point, you should probably bring Stephen Hawking into the conversation to bolster your side. Hawking, the smartest guy in the room, no matter what room he ever rolled into, developed a "no-boundary" proposal to describe the beginning of the universe. His "Hartle–Hawking state" (a theory he created with physicist James Hartle) describes a single starting point of space but no time, with nothing "before" because, as the theory goes, the universe is a closed loop. You could say that the Big Bang is the starting point the way the North Pole is the "start" of the Earth. But it's really just the northernmost point. There's nothing farther north, just like there's nothing before the Big Bang. In this way, the universe is completely self-contained, and

"there would be no need to specify behavior at the boundary. There would be no singularities at which the laws of science broke down and no edge of space-time at which one would have to appeal to God or some new law to set the boundary conditions for space-time... [The universe] would neither be created nor destroyed. It would just *be*."

This passage is from Hawking's landmark book, *A Brief History of Time*, and in the introduction to the book, world-renowned astronomer Carl Sagan put it more bluntly: "A universe with no edge in space, no beginning or end in time, and nothing for a Creator to do."

There are competing scientific theories of the universe, incidentally, such as the steady-state theory, string theory, something called "plasma cosmology," and the theory that a guy by the name of Biff Schlackenweiner created it in his garage one drunken night. But what the theories all have in common (except the Biff Schlackenweiner one, which I assure you I just made up, so don't go repeating it at a party to impress your friends) is that they are all just that—theories. The Hartle–Hawking state is not without its detractors. When it comes to the origin of the universe, *we just don't know*. None of us. Not you, not me, not the imposter at the valet stand, not even Stephen Hawking.

So where does that leave us? Well, I suggest we table the cosmological argument and, when we're better rested, circle back to it later. For now, let's move on to the next contestant on the list: *the teleological argument*. This argument, also referred to as "the argument from design," is another very popular argument, and it picks up where the cosmological argument ends. In other words, it's concerned with the way the universe proceeded *after* it came into existence.

The teleological argument has been around since the ancient Greeks.[6] In fact, we can credit Aristotle with the name, using, as he did, the Greek word *telos* to signify an aim, goal, or end. There is a goal for the universe, in other words. A plan. A design. But the argument was probably most famously summarized two thousand years later by English philosopher and clergyman William Paley

---

6. These were some smart dudes, huh? And as far as we know, not one of them had access to the internet.

(1743–1805), who made use of an analogy. In *Natural Theology or Evidences of the Existence and Attributes of the Deity* (1802), Paley, in so many words, wrote that a watch proves a watchmaker. If you were out strolling in the woods one day, so goes Paley's line of reasoning, and you spotted a pocket watch on the ground,[7] you'd pick it up and recognize immediately that it was not created accidentally. It's too complex and sophisticated. There are gears and springs and little wheels, and they all work together for a purpose. Obviously, it was carefully and meticulously *designed*.

So it is with the universe.

This argument has much to recommend it, starting with our observations of the world around us. Many great minds, including some pretty big scientific ones, have noted how unlikely it is that a universe like ours would evolve on its own in such a way as to form a planet that would, in turn, evolve in such a way as to form life that would, in turn, evolve in such a way as to become sentient and self-aware and even go on to become intelligent enough to start asking questions about the likelihood of our universe evolving as it has. You'll find no shortage of scientists to tell you that it's pretty much a miracle that we're here.

Okay, maybe that's a slight mischaracterization. Scientists don't often use words like "miracle" to describe things. But the fact is, there was a long list of conditions that needed to be met. For instance, physicist and professor Paul Davies (b. 1946) points out that if the force of the Big Bang (if you're relying on the Big Bang to explain existence) had been just a bit stronger or weaker, by a degree as tiny as one part in 10^{60} (!), stars (like our sun) would never have formed. In fact, as philosopher and author Jeffrey Koperski has

---

7. It's time for pocket watches to make a comeback, if you ask me. (And fedoras.)

pointed out, there were a bunch of parameters, including gravity, electromagnetism, strong and weak nuclear forces, and close to twenty more, that all needed to hit precise sweet spots to make this universe work as it does.

Not to mention the conditions necessary on planet Earth to allow life to form, and we're talking about *very* specific conditions, each needing to be *just right*. (In philosophical/scientific circles, you'll often hear this referred to as the "Goldilocks Principle.") Life needed the right temperature, the right atmospheric pressure, the right amount of water, the right amount of oxygen, the right ingredients in the proverbial primordial soup, and on and on and on. And if we hadn't had these, we wouldn't be here. You wouldn't be reading this book. (For which you might have been grateful. If you had existed, that is. Which you wouldn't have.) It all came together like, well, a finely tuned pocket watch.

I mean, think about this: life—animate, conscious, self-aware life—somehow arose from inanimate matter. That concept alone is breathtaking.

Many scientists have tried to calculate the odds of life spontaneously arising, and the odds are typically expressed as 1 in 10^x, where "x" is usually some really big-ass number, sometimes in the hundreds. Other scientists have put the matter more colorfully. British mathematician and astronomer Sir Fred Hoyle (1915–2001) once said that "the chance that higher life forms might have emerged (spontaneously) is comparable to the chance that a tornado sweeping through a junkyard might assemble a Boeing 747 from the materials therein." American biologist Edwin Conklin (1863–1952) said something similar: "The probability of life originating from accident is comparable to the probability of the Unabridged Dictionary resulting from an explosion in a printing factory."

It must be said, however, that while Conklin was a believer, Hoyle was an atheist. His quote is often used by theists, but the fact is that Hoyle believed not in an intelligent designer but in a theory called "panspermia," the idea that life originated somewhere else in the universe and traveled here by way of, say, asteroids, space dust, or even an alien spaceship. Of course, this only raises the question, How did *that* life originate? And then you're back to square one.

Now, as with the cosmological argument, this "intelligent design" argument, as you've probably seen it phrased these days, is not bulletproof. Atheists will point out that we have tons of data on things like tornadoes and Boeing 747s and explosions and unabridged dictionaries. We can legitimately calculate the odds for those types of things. But when it comes to the design of universes and what is required for a universe to produce life of some sort, we have only one from which to gather information, and one is a pretty dismal sample size. How can you assign odds to something when you have virtually no data? In fact, if you wanted to, you could turn the whole odds calculation thing on its head and argue this: in a sample of one universe, one universe evolved to produce life. Therefore, the odds are 100 percent in favor of universes producing life.

Atheists also argue that, as long as we're spit balling, why not postulate millions, billions, or even an infinite number of universes? Okay, they say, so maybe the near-impossible odds are accurate. Maybe it really is a billion-to-one shot. But how do we know there aren't a billion universes or more? Maybe none of the others evolved to produce life, but ours did. Not because of an intelligent designer but because there are so many universes. How about that, *hmmm*?

This is the so-called infinite monkey theorem. If you put an infinite number of monkeys behind an infinite number of computer keyboards, and they all randomly hit the keys an infinite number of times, eventually one of the monkeys is going to type out the complete works of Shakespeare, in which case you wouldn't need Shakespeare to explain the works of Shakespeare, just like you wouldn't need God to explain the existence of life if there were a billion (or an infinite number of) universes.

The problem with this theory, however, is math. Probability and statistics, to be precise. Every good probability and statistics student[8] knows that purely random events are independent of other events. It doesn't matter how many monkeys you have. It's the gambler's fallacy. You're playing poker, you're dealt a bunch of good hands in a row, and you believe you're on a hot streak. The next hand's going to be a winner, too. But the next hand has nothing to do with the previous hands. Do you know what the odds are of heads coming up after you toss a (legitimate) coin ninety-nine times, and tails has come up *every single time*? Fifty percent! Just like the odds on the very first toss. The result of the one-hundredth toss is unrelated to the prior ninety-nine.[9] Still, I suppose you could argue that an infinite number of monkeys is a lot of monkeys. Eventually, maybe one would at least type out one of the sonnets or maybe even *As You Like It*.

But that's all very theoretical. The better argument against the design idea is that we simply don't know enough about how universes evolve. And besides, it might be true that our universe is an amazing anomaly, but once begun, the evolution from inanimate

---

8. Not a description I was ever saddled with.

9. This is not to be confused with calculating the odds of heads coming up 100 times in a row. Considered as a set, the odds of 100 tosses coming up heads are extraordinarily low. But in considering each individual toss, the odds remain 50/50.

matter to life was, according to some experts, actually quite predictable. In his book *The Scientific Companion*, Italian-American geologist Cesare Emiliani (1922–1995) reminds us that evolution, in the form of Darwin's power of selection, was present even at the molecular level. "Given the chemical and environmental conditions of the primitive Earth," Emiliani says, "the appearance of life was a foregone conclusion. Only divine intervention could have kept Planet Earth sterile."

And some atheists, instead of arguing against design, actually use design as evidence *against* the existence of God. British philosopher Antony Flew (1923–2010), one of the foremost atheists of the twentieth century, did just this. He wondered why God, commonly thought of as all-powerful, would bother with such mundane processes as evolution. Why not just snap his omnipotent fingers and—boom—human life? Meanwhile, David Hume (even before Paley's time) asked, Is the universe really *that* well designed? Natural disasters, diseases, inefficiencies—what kind of designer is this?

Overall, however, I have to confess that, damn it, I *like* the teleological argument. I just do. It resonates with me. Sure, there are some bona fide objections to it, and if we're going to make a reasonable argument for God, those objections will have to be addressed. But this is not the time. This is the time to take a break. We could probably both use one. But let's make it short. I'm going to be back very soon (the page right after this one!) with the next chapter, where we will continue exploring this compelling list of arguments for the existence of a supreme being.

CHAPTER THREE

THE BIG 10: PART II

In our review of the ten major arguments in favor of the proposition that God exists, we've thus far examined three. The ontological argument essentially says that God exists because God is the greatest of all possible beings, and how could the greatest of all possible beings *not* exist? The cosmological argument reasons that the universe came into existence at some specific moment in the past, and since something cannot come out of nothing, then there must have been a prime mover responsible, i.e., God. Meanwhile, the teleological argument, or argument from design, proclaims that "a watch proves a watchmaker."

Personally, I like the second and third arguments, although I acknowledge that they are not without their objections.

This brings us to the fourth argument, which, interestingly, is a reply to one particular question that atheists are prone to ask: If there's a God, why has he not made himself known to us? There are actually a couple of different ways to answer this question, and we'll be addressing it later in the book as well. But for our purposes here, one common answer to the question is that God has, in fact, made himself known, thank you very much, and we have a *historical record* to prove it. And the historical record therefore proves God's existence.

What is this historical record? you ask. Well, there are several sources that history can draw upon. One of them begins, "In the beginning, God created the heavens and the earth." These words, the beginning passage of Genesis—the first book in the Old Testament, based largely on the Hebrew Bible—are *in print*. And we all know that if something is in print, then it must be true. Case closed.

Okay, so maybe we shouldn't be so quick to close this case. After all, nobody was around at the moment when the heavens and earth were created (even according to Genesis itself, man didn't come around for six more days, and when he did, he probably didn't have anything to write with), so this account of creation is hearsay at best.

Truthfully, nobody really knows the origin of the Old Testament, besides the fact that it is part of the Hebrew Bible. The Hebrew Bible—the Tanakh—is a collection of sacred scriptures that include subcollections called the Torah (which includes the first five books of the Old Testament, at one time believed to have been written by Moses himself), the Nevi'im, and the Ketuvim. And from where do these come? Well, chances are good that the material in these sacred writings, especially Genesis, represents a history that was passed down orally from generation to generation until writing was invented, and then onto parchment it went. But were the oral stories meant as factual accounts of the early days of humankind, or were they used instead for entertainment purposes around the newly invented campfire at the end of long days of hunting and gathering and running from saber-toothed tigers? Who can say.

Interestingly, many scholars have pointed out the similarities between Genesis and what's considered the oldest literary work in the history of humans, *The Epic of Gilgamesh*. This work, discovered in the historical region of Mesopotamia (somewhere around Iraq today), is believed to have been written around 2000 BCE and includes an Adam and Eve (Enkidu and Shamhat, respectively), a Garden of Eden motif, a snake, a temptation, and even a casting out. And there's a deluge story that suspiciously resembles the Genesis story of Noah's flood. Since it's believed that the Old Testament was committed to writing over a period of centuries starting around 1500 BCE (reaching its present form somewhere around 500 BCE), well after *The Epic of Gilgamesh*, it seems likely that at least some of the material was, shall we say, "borrowed" from *The Epic*, which is generally regarded as fiction anyway, since it's full of mythical characters like Ishtar (the goddess of love) and a terrible beast called the Bull of Heaven. Now, I suppose it *is* possible that the author of *The Epic of Gilgamesh* appropriated material from some oral story he might have overheard, a story that would eventually be written down as Genesis. So who took from whom? Which came first? Adam and Eve or Enkidu and Shamhat? Maybe it doesn't matter. Let's face it: the Genesis account of creation, by itself—even if original—reads a heck of a lot like myth.

Now, as the Old Testament continues beyond Genesis, we have accounts of God's interaction with man that could have taken place after people were writing things down. Many scholars believe Moses, or at least someone very much like Moses as described in the Old Testament, might have actually existed around 1300 BCE, when pieces of the Old Testament could have been in their early, rough-draft form. But, alas, the evidence of a connection between a possible archeological Moses and the biblical Moses who supposedly parted the Red Sea is pretty scant. And it should be said that the evidence for God's supposed revelation of himself to other Old Testament figures, including the likes of Abraham, Jacob, Joseph, David, Elijah, and Bob, is pretty thin, too.[1]

Furthermore, many scholars have pointed out that besides *The Epic of Gilgamesh*, other ancient texts include flood stories or other stories that are awfully darn close to stories like what you'll find in the Old Testament about Solomon, Samson, Isaac, and others. Some even feel that the Ten Commandments in the book of Exodus could well have been taken from the Code of Hammurabi, a Babylonian legal text written about a thousand years *before* Exodus.

Now, for my money, things get much more interesting in the New Testament, when God not only supposedly revealed himself to humans but became one. The gospels tell us that Jesus was God incarnate. But it's important to understand that there are different gospels. The *canonical gospels*—Matthew, Mark, Luke, and John—are accounts of Jesus's life and are designated canonical because they made it into the official canon—the New Testament itself. (The books of the New Testament were formally canonized in 393 CE at the Council of Hippo in northern Africa, just in case you were wondering.)

Matthew, Mark, and Luke, specifically, are referred to as *synoptic gospels*, from the Latin *synopsis*, meaning "a seeing altogether." These three gospels, written between 66 and 85 CE, are really close in subject matter, telling many of the same stories about Jesus in slightly different ways. In fact, the similarities being so close has given rise to what's known as the "synoptic problem." Have these three gospels relied on each other for source material? Maybe. Instead of three wholly independent accounts, it seems at least

---

1. Ha! Just seeing if you're still paying attention. There's really no "Bob" in the Old Testament.

possible that someone might have copied his buddy's homework. Not that there's anything necessarily wrong with this. It's generally believed that Mark was the first gospel written, and it's perfectly understandable that Matthew and Luke might have relied on Mark's version to confirm some details while supplementing the material with their own stuff. Why reinvent the wheel?

Now, John has some of the same stories, too, but John gets a little more into the theology of Jesus, doing a deeper dive into what his life and death presumably meant. Of course, there is more to the New Testament besides the gospels, much of it written by the apostle Paul, an interesting figure in his own right. Paul never knew Jesus in Jesus's lifetime but famously converted to the way of Jesus (in fact, before it was called Christianity, it was simply called "The Way") on the road to Damascus one day.

But even the four gospels were not written contemporaneously with Jesus's life. And they were also written anonymously. The names were assigned to the works maybe a century after they were written, and they were all written well after Jesus's death.

There are other gospels that never made it into the canon, ending up on the proverbial cutting room floor, if you will. There are gospels attributed to people with names like Marcion, Philip, Bartholomew, and even a gospel attributed to—get this—Mary Magdalene. There's a Secret Gospel of Mark and a Gospel of Peter that comes with a story of a walking, talking cross. Some gospels were discovered after the Council of Hippo in 393 and had no chance of being canonized. *Way* after. A slew of ancient texts, including the provocative Gospel of Thomas and the Gospel of Truth, were discovered in the town of Nag Hammadi in Egypt in 1945. Talk about an archeological find!

These all give varying perspectives on Jesus, some of which aren't exactly in precise accord with the canonical gospels. The

Gospel of Philip, for instance, talks of a possible romantic relationship between Jesus and Mary Magdalene. The Gospel of Thomas delivers not a narrative but 114 sayings of Jesus and implies that personal salvation comes from understanding the "secret" knowledge of these sayings.

What do all these gospels—canonical and non-canonical, with their similarities and differences, found in different parts of the ancient world, and written by different hands at different times—collectively mean? Well, they mean that there was obviously a shitload of interest in this person named Jesus, and it might be worth asking why. It's hard to imagine all these accounts being written about a fictional person, but is there an argument for the historicity of Jesus? Well, present-day scholars are basically certain that Jesus was a historical person, so it would be more appropriate to ask if there's an argument *against* the historicity of Jesus. Besides the gospels, which many believe are historical accounts, Jesus was written about by first-century historians Flavius Josephus and Publius Cornelius Tacitus, who, apart from having kickass names, are generally regarded as primo historians. And there were others. In fact, theologian Graham Stanton (1940–2009) has written that "there is general agreement that, with the possible exception of Paul, we know far more about Jesus of Nazareth than about any first or second century Jewish or pagan religious teacher."

Ah, but let us not lose sight of the question we are asking. It's one thing to claim that this man known as Jesus of Nazareth existed. It's another thing to claim that *God* exists. Can one draw a line from Jesus to God? Does the former prove the latter? It does if you believe that Jesus was God incarnate or, at the very least, a messenger of God who, when he was executed, rose from the dead and now "is seated at the right hand of God the Father almighty," as the Apostles' Creed puts it. But here is where the historical evidence begins to thin out a bit. We may know Jesus existed, but we don't know exactly what he said. And even if we believed he said the things attributed to him (as written in the gospels), how can we know what he said was true?

Believing in Jesus as God incarnate, if you don't believe in God, doesn't make a lot of sense. It's backward. You'd need to believe in God first. Then, maybe, there would be an argument for Jesus's divinity. Which is to say that perhaps we should put a pin in the New Testament discussion at this point. I have to confess that I find the Jesus story endlessly intriguing. His birth, his death, the message, the ethic—it's all pretty amazing. Have you ever read the Sermon on the Mount? I mean, you've heard of it, but have you actually read it? Borrow someone's Bible and read Matthew 5–7. (Right now. I'll wait.) Nevertheless, the story of Jesus clearly loses some of its luster if God doesn't exist. I happen to think it's worth a closer look, but perhaps now is not the time.

So are there other historical documents that can point us toward God? Actually, there are a bunch. Muslims, for example, believe that the 114 chapters of the Quran are a revelation from God. These revelations were supposedly passed directly from God to the prophet Muhammad. The Quran was written between 610 and 632 CE and, in fact, mentions the Hebrew Bible and the gospels. It includes many of the same characters that are in the Old and New Testaments, including Moses and Jesus.

Hinduism has its sacred texts as well, such as the Vedas, thought to have been written in roughly the same time frame as the Old Testament. These scriptures are believed by Hindus to have been sourced in eternal knowledge and transmitted to humans via enlightened sages. There are texts relevant to Buddhism, Taoism, Shinto, Zoroastrianism, Jainism, and about a thousand other religions and offshoots of religions. Some of these reference God, or different names of God, or the gods (plural), and some make no reference to God at all.

Of course, we're only concerned with those that claim to be revelations of God, thereby providing evidence of God's existence. But the direct revelation claims of sacred texts like the Hebrew Bible, the New Testament, the Quran, the Vedas—well, they all suffer from the same problem, of course. The problem of verifiability. They were all written centuries and centuries ago, mostly from oral traditions that began God-knows-how-many centuries before that. The witnesses to these revelations are long gone.

It might be worth asking, however, since we're talking about historical evidence of God, if there are any outside historical sources, evidence from impartial authorities, that may confirm these sacred texts. We already mentioned the historians Josephus and Tacitus, but they were little help beyond supporting the idea that a certain religious teacher named Jesus existed. But might there be archeological evidence that can help substantiate the stories of these texts?

Well, here's something interesting. Although historians figure that the Old Testament, particularly the first five books (the Hebrew Torah), were finalized somewhere around 500 BCE, the oldest extant copies—that is to say, the oldest copies still in existence—only date back to the tenth century CE, a full fifteen hundred years after they were supposedly written.[2] At least those *used* to be the oldest extant copies. But in 1946 came another stunning archeological find, this one on the north shore of the Dead Sea—the aptly named "Dead Sea Scrolls." The dig went on

---

2. So how do we know when they were originally written? Historians consider a lot of factors, including references to historical events, styles of writing, and linguistic clues. Just like a thousand years from now, when an archeologist comes across a copy of a text that uses the word "groovy," they'll be able to say, "Hey, this was originally written in the 1960s!"

for a decade, uncovering copies of such biblical books as Genesis, Exodus, Psalms, Isaiah, Daniel, the Song of Songs, and a bunch more. The scrolls were dated to the second century BCE, a *thousand years* before the next oldest copies we have of these books.

But here's the really amazing part. The texts of the books were almost identical to the next oldest copies, meaning that over the course of those thousand years, the transmission of the text from copy to copy was extraordinarily accurate. You know that telephone game you played as a kid where you line up and pass a whispered message down the line? It starts out as something like, "My little kitten loves milk," and by the time it gets to the last kid, the message is something like, "Leave the gun, take the cannoli."[3] Well, that didn't happen here. For instance, as Hebrew scholar Millar Burrows has noted, "Of the 166 *words* in Isaiah 53, there are only seventeen *letters* in question." And none of them affect the meaning. Over a thousand years!

What does this tell us? Well, for what it's worth, it suggests that the Bible hasn't changed much since its original writing. And so perhaps we shouldn't be too quick to dismiss it because of age. It's probable that the Dead Sea Scrolls, like the newer extant copies, were accurate written transcriptions of stories that were told, or written, centuries before. This doesn't make them true, of course. But it's interesting to consider the amount of care that was taken with these books over the centuries, the obvious desire to get them right, to preserve the integrity of the original messages therein. True or not, these are obviously important documents in the history of humankind.

Which is why we've spent a whole chapter on biblical texts. We need to understand their importance. Entire religions are based on

---

3. *The Godfather*, 1972.

them. What is Christianity without the New Testament? What is Islam without the Quran? Just how much importance to ascribe to these texts is up to you. Yes, they are significant in the history of humankind, but are they accurate *accounts* of the history of humankind? That's a big question. We're probably not at a point where we can say that the biblical record proves God. But what remains to be seen (this author adds cryptically) is whether God can prove the biblical record.

Chapter Four

The Big 10: Part III

I n the last chapter, we were reminded of how important biblical (or sacred or religious) texts are in any discussion of the existence of God, not just to present-day people but also to the ancients, who—at least some evidence suggests—read the exact same texts as we do today. Entire religions are based on these texts, and adherents of these religions will tell you that the texts prove God.

I think that's a big step, but I also think we should at least remain open to *some* connection between these texts and the possible existence of God. You might disagree, but—for now—that's okay. We're moving on anyway.

And so, without further ado, I present to you *the moral argument for God*. Many philosophers and theologians, including one of Christianity's greatest all-time defenders, C. S. Lewis (1898–1963), otherwise of *The Chronicles of Narnia* fame, have observed that nowhere in nature do you find any sort of morality. And so if nature doesn't provide it, there must be a supernatural source for it. C. S. Lewis made a lot of arguments for God, but this was his go-to.

He wasn't the first. Saint Thomas Aquinas put an argument together in his *Summa Theologica*. He believed that there are different levels of morality, and this makes some intuitive sense. We all know people who are immoral and that some are more immoral than others, just as we know some people who are good people and some people who are *really* good people, the kind of people you always feel as though you have to watch your language around. The kind of people to whom you'd never admit that you watch Jerry Springer reruns or that more than once you've eaten an entire package of cookie dough (one time while watching a Jerry Springer rerun). Aquinas asserted that if we know there are gradations of morality, then there must be some perfect standard of morality. After all, what would the gradations otherwise be based on? There's a standard, and then there are levels at varying distances below the standard. A perfect standard implies God.

Besides being a claim for God, the idea that morality is somehow inherent in the universe is also a claim that morality originates from outside the human mind. This is no small thought. It's a little more than just saying that it comes from God. Morality exists, so the argument goes, *independently* of human experience or beliefs. The idea that concepts like morality exist with or without us is something we're going to examine further a little later on. It might sound far-fetched to you now (especially if you don't believe in God), but keep it in mind. We'll table it for now and instead address the moral argument with its most common objection: moral beliefs are nicely explained by evolution.

It's hard to object to this objection. As humans developed and formed themselves into societies (for safety, procreation, and other reasons, like karaoke night around the campfire), it became necessary for survival (of an individual and, indeed, the species) to get along. It was a sociological evolution. To cooperate. To befriend. To pull together. To shout out, "Hey, Chuck, look out, there's a saber-toothed tiger behind you!" instead of just sitting there watching Chuck get devoured. And, of course, Chuck would repay you by making you a nice mammoth burger that evening, really lean, just the way you like it, served with a tasty beer.[1] This dynamic makes perfect sense to me.

Theists have a habit of turning to atheists and making arguments like, "Well, if God doesn't exist, what's to keep you from doing anything you want? *Well? Huh?*" as if the threat of divine punishment is all that's keeping us from murdering and raping each other. That's pretty weak. I always cringe when I see a believer present this question as an irrefutable argument. (It also makes me wonder just what the believer *really* wants to do that their belief in God is keeping them from doing. If they were suddenly convinced God didn't exist, would they murder and rape? Are these theists just psychopaths prevented from committing atrocities only by their belief in God? Let's hope they never deconvert, huh?)

On the other hand, let's consider a story that Joseph Campbell (1904–1987), famed writer, professor, and lifelong student of myth, related to journalist Bill Moyers during a series of interviews in 1988.[2] Campbell talked about a police officer who saved a young man who was about to throw himself off a tall cliff in Hawaii. There was a mountain road that ran past this particular spot, and the officer was driving by with his partner when he spotted the young man. He jumped out of the car, ran to the man, and grabbed him just as the man was taking a leap. Fortunately, the

---

1. This is entirely possible. The Sumerians were making beer in 4000 BCE. Of course, mammoths went extinct around 10000 BCE, but it's still possible that somebody might have been making beer back then. I like to think so. Life was tough enough in those days without the added difficulty of not having something to quench a guy's thirst after a long day.

2. These interviews became a PBS series called "The Power of Myth" that I *highly* recommend.

second cop came up and grabbed the first cop just in the nick of time, or the first cop would have gone over the cliff with the young man, whom he never surrendered his grip on.

The first cop was hailed as a hero for saving the young man's life, and when he was asked by a reporter why he didn't just let go and instead risked his own life (which surely would have been lost without his partner's quick action), he said, "I couldn't let go. If I had let that young man go, I couldn't have lived another day of my life."

What explains this? What explains why people go into burning buildings to save strangers? What explains *sacrifice?* Duty alone? Campbell had another explanation. At the moment when the cop latched onto the man, every thought other than the thought of saving the man was gone from his head. Campbell called it a moment of "one-pointed meditation." No shit, huh? Nothing else mattered. Why? Because in that moment, with everything else stripped away, the cop *saw himself in the young man.*

This idea of seeing ourselves in the other is essentially a non-evolutionary argument for why we have morality. Although evolution might explain shouting out a warning to Chuck, it doesn't quite explain risking your life for him if he were jumping off a cliff. Or, for that matter, even warning him about that saber-toothed tiger. In fact, evolution, sourced in survival, would better explain the opposite action, wouldn't it? Let the saber-toothed tiger devour Chuck, thus giving you time to run the hell away. Cripes, you can make your own beer. You don't need Chuck. What's Chuck ever done for you?

Among those in the evolutionary field, this apparent paradox has a name. It's called *the problem of altruism*, and Charles Darwin himself acknowledged that this seeming paradox was potentially fatal to his whole theory of natural selection. How is sacrifice explained by evolution? Scientists have one theory, although it is by no means universally agreed upon. W. D. Hamilton (1936–2000), British evolutionary biologist, postulated something known as "Hamilton's rule," which deals with the concept of kin selection and essentially says that it's within an organism's best interest, from a species standpoint, to sacrifice for one's close relation if the reproductive benefit of doing so (carrying on the genes of the sacrificer) outweighs the cost of the sacrifice. It's a calculation. (He actually created a formula, which I see little reason to reproduce here.) And so Darwin's selection process means that the genes of those organisms who have sacrificed for their offspring are passed along, including the gene that decided to make the sacrifice. Fellow evolutionary biologist Richard Dawkins, whom we'll be hearing more from later, calls this the "selfish gene." It's not altruism at all, and therefore there's no paradox.

I submit that this seems like a stretch. There were no such calculations being made on that cliff in Hawaii. It's possible, of course, that over eons, the selfish gene sort of took on a life of its own, expanding to encompass a concern, even empathy, for not only offspring and kin but for humankind in general. "We" becomes stronger than "me." It could also be argued that the cliff example is an anomaly. Maybe most people would have let go of the young man. I don't know. For now, I'm just going to say that I find the discussion pretty interesting and relevant. From whence comes morality? The answer somehow seems important to our overall discussion.

We're going to dispense with the next argument rather quickly, not because it's not legitimate but because I have a feeling that *you* won't find it legitimate, and so we're probably better off focusing our efforts elsewhere. *The existential argument for God* basically says that we *need* to believe. Human beings require meaning in their lives. We need to know that there are reasons for things, especially bad things, even if those reasons remain hidden. We need security. We need to know that there's a purpose for the world and a purpose for life and that maybe life doesn't end with death; maybe there's something more.

In some ways, this is an argument of pragmatism, and you *cannot* talk about pragmatism without invoking the name William James (1842–1910), a giant mind of philosophy and psychology of the late-nineteenth to early-twentieth century. James, with Charles Sanders Peirce (1839–1914), pretty much invented the philosophical school of thought known as "pragmatism." We touched on this earlier in our discussion of truth. According to pragmatism, truthfulness can be judged by its degree of usefulness. And so, if a belief in God is useful, if it gives meaning to life, if it provides purpose and security and maybe peace of mind, then damn it, why not just believe? Those are good reasons to believe, aren't they? True, they're not *evidentiary* reasons. But they're practical, beneficial reasons. And for many people, that's enough.

John Stuart Mill (1806–1873), a prominent ethicist, political theorist,[3] and, more importantly for us, an agnostic and a skeptic, once wrote, "It appears to me that the indulgence of hope with regard to the government of the universe and the destiny of man after death, while we recognize as a clear truth that we have no grounds for more than a hope, is legitimate and philosophically defensible." Hope is enough, even according to this famous agnostic.

But I'm aware it's probably not enough for you. You need a better justification for believing in God than need or hope.

---

3. He was big on individual rights, and if you've ever heard of the concept of the "tyranny of the majority," that was Mill.

Well, what about the threat of missing out on eternal life, or, worse, being consigned to eternal damnation? Are you willing to bet your eternal life on your belief that God does not exist? That's a question Blaise Pascal (1623–1662), French philosopher (and physicist and mathematician),[4] asked in his posthumously published *Pensées* ("Thoughts"). The proposition has since become referred to as *Pascal's wager*, and it's the next argument for us to consider.[5]

Pascal noted that everyone has to choose. You either believe in God (and presumably live your life accordingly), or you do not. It's a wager. But if you choose to believe in God, you have everything to gain (eternal life) and very little to lose (maybe you give up a few superficial luxuries, like sleeping in on Sundays). If, on the other hand, you choose not to believe in God, you have everything to lose (no eternal life or, worse, eternal life in Hell) and very little to win. And so to Pascal, it was a no-brainer. You'd have to be an idiot not to believe. This is what we might call standard decision theory today. Note that Pascal wasn't necessarily making an argument for the existence of God (even though we're including it here) so much as making an argument for *believing* in God.

Pascal's wager has faced criticism over the years, as you might imagine. Some philosophers have wondered at what kind of belief it really is if it's basically manufactured because you don't want to take the chance of ending up in Hell. French Enlightenment philosopher Voltaire (1694–1778) called the wager "indecent and childish." He thought the argument was weak, and he might have

---

4. All these big-brained guys seemed to do more than one thing, didn't they? I'm guessing you probably couldn't make a living just from philosophy.

5. My favorite quote from Blaise Pascal: "All of humanity's problems stem from man's inability to sit quietly in a room alone." Right?

had a point. How sincere is your faith, really, if all you're doing is paying it lip service, carrying it around out of fear like a Get Out of Hell Free card? Other thinkers have asked, "Which God?" noting that different religions have different definitions. Pascal was Catholic, but maybe eternal salvation is found elsewhere, perhaps in the Hindu god Vishnu.

So why, you're asking, am I including Pascal's wager in a list of arguments for the existence of God? Pascal himself never intended his wager to be evidence for God. In fact, he felt that God could not be found with reason alone in arguments such as those we are advancing here, or at least he maintained that an argument based on reason wouldn't hold water for someone determined not to believe.[6]

Ah, but that is the point, you see. Let's take another look at these last two arguments: one that says that hope and need are sufficient reasons to believe in God, and one that says, essentially, that you've got nothing to lose by believing, and potentially much to gain. In some sense, both of these arguments are starting points for something larger, something more significant. Augustine of Hippo (354–430) was an extraordinarily influential father of the Christian church. Remember the Council of Hippo, where the New Testament was formally canonized? Augustine was there. (He was probably the keynote speaker.) Augustine wrote some very important works that collectively had a huge impact on the development of Christian doctrine at an extraordinarily crucial time in the church's early history, including *On Christian Doctrine* (397 CE) and *Confessions* (400 CE), the latter an autobiographical account where Augustine divulged the details of his sinful and

---

6. He actually put it this way: "There is light enough for those who wish to see, and darkness enough for those who are otherwise inclined."

immoral youth. Apparently, he was quite the libertine. But he converted to Christianity, and his book expresses much philosophical and spiritual insight, so much so that it's thought of today as one of the great works in the history of religious philosophy. In fact, Ludwig Wittgenstein (1889–1951), one of the twentieth century's greatest philosophers, called *Confessions* "the most serious book ever written."

All of which is to say that Augustine was a damn fine theologian–philosopher. Ultimately, he would go on to become a saint and have a lovely town on the east coast of Florida named in his honor.[7] Anyway, among all the things Augustine said and wrote, one of his most significant declarations was this: "Unless you believe, you will not understand." He sort of borrowed this thought from *Isaiah* in the Old Testament, but he expanded on it. Augustine's doctrine of "divine illumination" essentially says that understanding is provided by God. Human reasoning is insufficient. But to acquire divine understanding, one must first believe in God. Faith, Augustine is saying, *precedes* reason.

If one accepts the existential argument for God based on need or hope and/or takes Pascal's wager and bets on God, then understanding will follow. Think of it as being more open-minded to information that may come down the pike to shine a brighter light on the whole God question. It's like being put in the right mood. You may be more meditative or more reflective, perhaps more inclined to "see" or "hear" or otherwise sense God's presence in the universe, maybe even in your own life.

Inclined, you say, or predisposed and susceptible? Isn't this a lot like believing what you want to believe and seeing what you want

---

7. And promptly mispronounced. The saint: aw-*gust*-in. The city: *aw*-gə-steen.

to see? Well, maybe. But I'm glad you asked, because this brings us rather nicely to our next argument for God.

CHAPTER FIVE

THE BIG 10: PART IV

A fter discussing the moral argument for God in the last chapter and presenting the attendant problem of altruism for
those deferring to evolution, we talked about the existential argument, which suggests that it's okay to believe based on one's need
to believe. Pascal's wager took a slightly different approach, saying
more or less that it's okay to believe out of FOMO—fear of missing
out. However one gets to the position of belief, Augustine argues
that the position is a necessary starting point for understanding
God, which is kind of backward from having God revealed to you
and then deciding to believe. But what exactly is this understanding we speak of?

Well, some people will tell you that it includes a sense, as mentioned in the last chapter, of God's presence. And this lands us
right on the doorstep of our next argument for God's existence: *the
prevalence of religious experience*. I noted in Chapter 1 that around
half the US public has copped to having had some form of religious
or mystical or spiritual experience in their lives. Numbers are similar throughout the world.[1] I also suggested that any one particular

---

1. I can't back that up, but it seems reasonable, doesn't it? Maybe more so in
   more religious societies, maybe less so in more secular ones. Either way, there's
   a shitload of people who claim to have had these experiences.

person's description of such an experience isn't something we can really use as evidence of God's existence. Direct awareness is too personal to be transmissible to someone else.

But can we consider religious experiences *collectively*? Look, if 99 percent of the people in the world told you that bees make honey, wouldn't you believe them? Even if you had never personally witnessed it happening (or ever researched the process yourself, or asked experts, like beekeepers)? In fact, you probably never *have* seen bees making honey, have you? But you believe it, even with no firsthand knowledge, right? And you believe it because there are a lot of sources that have confirmed it.

There's a difference here, of course. First, we don't have 99 percent of the population attesting to having had an experience they would classify as religious. We have roughly 50 percent. Second, the information being passed along on religious experience is highly subjective and widely variable. Beekeeper A and Beekeeper B would describe the process of honey-making in very similar ways. So would Beekeepers C, D, and E. The process is always the same. It's reproducible. Not so with religious experiences, which seem to fluctuate wildly from person to person and cannot generally be impartially witnessed.

Nevertheless, 50 percent of the population saying anything even remotely the same seems worth considering, doesn't it? Maybe, in the end, you'll reject everything that 50 percent has said, but it seems to me as though it's worth at least investigating, no?

But what do we mean by a "religious" experience? The Pew survey mentioned above phrased it like this: "a religious or mystical experience—that is, a moment of religious or spiritual awakening." German philosopher Friedrich Schleiermacher (1768–1834) wrote about religious experience as feeling and intuition, a sense of what he called "absolute dependence," a conscious feeling of being in relation to God. Another German thinker by the name of Rudolf Otto (1869–1937) wrote of "numinous" experiences and suggested that they had three ingredients: first, they are experiences unlike any other; second, they evoke silence and even terror; and third, they are fascinating, compelling, and even marked by grace.

But I don't know if we want to pigeonhole experiences that a lot of people have trouble finding words for. Let's just say there are varieties of religious experience, and for a closer look into the subject, you could do a lot worse than consulting (naturally) *The Varieties of Religious Experience*, a classic of Western philosophy and psychology by our favorite pragmatist, William James. This book, taken from a series of lectures from 1901–1902 and still in print to this day, details many examples of religious experience from a psychological perspective. James never actually says whether he believes that the experiences he details were real, but he suggests that they might be *true* in the pragmatic sense of the word; that is, they were *useful* to the people who had them.

The upshot is that this book got a lot of people talking about religious experiences. We often think of such experiences as being really significant, momentous events. Burning bushes, being levitated, experiencing a bona fide miracle, etc. But James speaks of more mundane experiences. Hearing a voice, perhaps, that induces a change for the better in one's behavior or seeing some sign that seems to herald an improvement in health or financial circumstances.

It's these smaller experiences that I find interesting. Many people never hear a voice or see a sign but merely feel a presence, one that they ascribe to "the divine" or something "transcendent." This "transcendent" idea is the key, it seems to me, pointing as it does to something *beyond* the experiencer, as though the experiencer is in some form of union with something *outside* of themselves. Indeed, *transcendence* appears to be the common denominator of religious experience in that people believe the experience (the presence or voice or sign or whatever) was sourced in something not of the material world. In fact, I would suggest that transcendence is a necessary component of a religious experience.

We've all heard of this kind of experience, of course. People talk of somehow moving beyond their physical bodies in prayer or meditation or in moments of acute crisis or even great pain (or ecstatic pleasure). Music, dance, and even extreme exercise (think "runner's high") are all moments that you'll hear people speak of transcendence. And, of course, people (not me, mind you) have felt such moments while on psychotropic drugs.

Maybe you've experienced such out-of-body moments yourself but never ascribed them to something beyond yourself. Maybe you feel that such experiences are all just in the head of the experiencer. You would not be alone in this belief. Sigmund Freud (speaking of giants of psychology), a relative contemporary of James, believed that religious experiences were essentially hallucinations, the manifestations of subconscious wish fulfillment. (With Freud, *everything* is to be explained by the subconscious.) God, to Freud, was a fantasy, a result of our primitive need for a father figure. Moreover, we know today that the brain is capable of producing feel-good chemicals that create euphoric mental states.

I would just say this: it's extraordinarily difficult to persuade someone who's convinced they've had a transcendent experience that it was all just a hallucination, mere wish-fulfillment based on their "fantasy" that God exists, or a brain-created chemical high. To use what we learned in Chapter 1, someone who's had an experience they would define as "a moment of religious or spiritual awakening" would be well within their epistemological rights to claim justified true belief—knowledge!—of God.

We also know from Chapter 1 that there is room for skepticism, even with justified true belief. Nevertheless, if half the people in the US believe they've had some sort of religious experience, that's 165 million people. And here's the thing: to use religious experience as a halfway decent argument for God, only one of them—*one person in 165 million*—has to relate a story of an experience that accurately represents reality. For if one story of transcendence is real, then it's time to rethink everything. If transcendence is possible, then that suggests that there is more to the universe than the material world. You can't move "out of body" unless there is something to move *to*.

Would this, in and of itself, prove God? Maybe not. But it would prove that there is more to the universe than materialism, and that's at least a step in the direction of God. For now, however, we'll let the matter rest. You can decide for yourself whether 165 million people have been victims of hallucinations while we move on to the next argument, which, interestingly, is closely tied to this last one. For if a theist is going to postulate something beyond materialism, then why not use, as prima facie evidence, human consciousness? And hence we arrive at *mind–body dualism*, otherwise referred to as the argument from consciousness.

Human consciousness is a problem to explain. I don't mean this frivolously, as in "My neighbor's choice of presidential candidate is a problem to explain."[2] Nor am I referring to degree of difficulty, as in "Linear algebra is a problem to explain." What I mean is that *we can't explain* how human consciousness works. More precisely, we can't explain *experience*. In fact, explaining consciousness is such a hard problem that philosophers (creative and imaginative

---

2. But it really is. And why doesn't he mow his lawn more often?

characters that they are) have come to call it "the hard problem of consciousness."

This, in contrast to "the easy problem of consciousness." "The easy problem" refers to the ways in which the brain works: the mechanics of how we sense things, how we process information, and how we feel, think, and react. Science is pretty good with this "how" stuff. The hard problem is still a head-scratcher. David Chalmers (b. 1966), a big-brained guy who specializes in philosophy of mind and is a professor of philosophy and neural science at New York University, introduced the term "hard problem" in a 1995 paper. Chalmers asks about our experience of, well, experience. The brain feeds us data to process, right? Let's say the data is a really sad song. Think of the saddest song you've ever heard. Maybe it makes you sad enough to want to cry.[3] The question is, why do you feel like you want to cry? Why do you feel sad? Why do you *feel* anything at all?

There's nothing we can find in the physical world that accounts for this phenomenon. There's nothing that accounts for the fact that we experience things. There's no universal agreement on what it even means to experience something. Moreover, there's no evolutionary process that can explain how consciousness rose from matter so that we can experience anything at all. We might (*might*, I say) be able to explain how the brain *physically* evolved, but we can't explain how it jumped from the physical to the conscious. In fact, how could our brains have even evolved physically if consciousness wasn't present in the first place to inform us through our *experiencing* of the world and thus guide us in such a way that we could survive and, presumably, evolve?

---

3. YouTube the High Kings's version of "Green Fields of France," if you're stuck for one. My goodness.

All of this seemingly points toward dualism, the belief that the mind is separate from the body, which is to say, it is separate from the physical world. We can thank one of our favorite rationalists, René Descartes, for bringing this belief to the forefront of Western philosophy way before Chalmers.[4] In fact, the matter is often referred to as "Cartesian dualism." It seemed obvious to Descartes that the mind is a non-physical entity. There are, he believed, the physical and the mental.

But fast forward a few hundred years, and it's clear that we have a much greater understanding of the connection between the mind and the body, right? In fact, a strict materialist will tell you that there really is no such thing as the mind, outside of a means by which to describe mental phenomena like thought and emotion and sensation and memory and imagination, etc. In other words, it's just a word used to describe certain things that the *brain* does. But it has no place in the real world. Thoughts, feelings, and sensations are just brain events. There's nothing more to the story. Our latest understandings of the working of the brain answer everything quite satisfactorily, thank you very much. There's only the brain, a part of our body. Even Descartes, if he were around today, would have to agree.

Not so fast, my friend. Remember, that's the easy problem. The mechanics. The "how." The hard problem persists. The phenomenon of experience itself. Not how we experience, but why experiencing exists, or what, in its essence, it even is. We don't have a (materialistic, scientific) theory to explain it. Descartes's ideas are evidently alive and well.[5]

---

4. Though, once again, the ancient Greeks had already given the issue some serious consideration.

5. Even though Descartes himself ceased being alive and well in 1650.

Interesting aside: back in 1998, at the annual meeting of the Association for the Scientific Study of Consciousness, David Chalmers made a bet for a case of wine with a noted neuroscientist named Christof Koch. Koch bet that within twenty-five years, science would have a clear explanation for consciousness. Chalmers said no way. In 2023—twenty-five years later—in front of an audience at New York University, Koch presented Chalmers with his case of wine. Science still had no clear explanation. But before the evening ended, Chalmers asked for double or nothing. In 2048, they'll meet again (Koch will be ninety-one, and Chalmers will be eighty-two). My suspicion is that Chalmers will collect another case of wine.

Here's another (not so small) thing: when we say we experience something, what exactly is meant by *we*? Or to make it more personal, *I*. When you say, "I feel sad when I hear this song," what are you referring to with the subject "I"? What does "I" mean?

To put it another way, just who is the brain working for? What is this entity that is busy processing the data being supplied and is thus consequently experiencing life? The experiences belong to somebody, right? A self? A. G. Cairns-Smith, in his fascinating *Evolving the Mind: On the Nature of Matter and the Origin of Consciousness*, tells a story of famed molecular biologist Francis Crick trying to explain why it's so difficult to understand how we can perceive anything at all. But someone listening to his explanation said she didn't have any real problem with the idea; she just pictured something like a little television set inside her head. Apparently, she was left speechless when Crick asked, "So who is looking at it?"

Some big thinkers deny the existence of the self. Hume had a "bundle theory," in which he defined the self as a sort of collection of experiences, a cohesion of related perceptions that are always changing. But the relation of past experiences gives the impression that there's a constant, enduring, singular identity present. A self. But alas, there's not. The self, according to Hume (or rather, the bundle of experiences we call Hume), is an illusion.

Interestingly, his theory is pretty darn close to the Buddhist concept of the no-self. We are constantly in flux, you see. You're different from who you were a year ago, an hour ago, even from the moment you began reading this sentence. It's the idea of not being able to step into the same river twice. What sense can it make to talk of some underlying permanent self? Yesterday's "self" is different, by no matter how small a degree, from today's. Just when you think you've got the self pinned down, it has become something else.

Daniel Dennett (b. 1942), famous philosopher and scientist and ardent atheist, denies the self as well. In fact, he denies consciousness, thus solving in one fell swoop the hard problem thereof.[6] The concept is an abstraction in Dennett's view, so why all the fuss? It's an illusion. In fact, there's a whole philosophical train of thought called illusionism that contends that consciousness is a figment of the brain's imagination.

Me, I happen think it's worth wondering about consciousness and this "self" thing. Aren't *you* more than your brain? More than neurons firing? More than chemical processes? More than an abstract bundle of related experiences? Don't *you* feel pain? Didn't *you* "borrow" your mom's car when you were sixteen without asking? But if so, where is this *you*? Science has done a lot

---

6. Well, technically, he doesn't outwardly deny it, but noted philosopher John Searle has accused him of doing so, and the two have had a rather colorful spat going on about it. Suffice it to say that Dennett's definition isn't one you or I would recognize as describing what's typically meant by consciousness.

with the brain, but science has never discovered a person in one, complete with all their memories, experiences, and personality quirks. It seems at least possible that the mind is real and that the mind transcends the brain. And hey, look, there's that word again. "Transcend."

Of course, even if the mind exists and is separate from the physical world, that still doesn't prove God. That only proves that there's some aspect of reality that lies beyond matter. But it gets interesting if you combine these last two arguments. If people who've reported religious experiences have somehow found something in this non-material world of reality we call consciousness, something that has made them come away with "a moment of religious or spiritual awakening," then maybe those experiences, in that world of non-material reality, are connections to something *else* present in the world of non-material reality, something capable of producing—*of all experiences*—spiritual ones. Maybe... God?

Well, maybe. If consciousness exists. If we're more than a bundle of loosely related experiences that our physical brains have somehow cobbled together into a convenient fiction that we call, for lack of a better word, the self. (And if everybody's not hallucinating.)

I'll let you mull over exactly what *your* self is while we make our way to our final stop on the argument-for-God tour: *the aesthetic argument*, sometimes called "the argument from beauty." Now, instead of a sad song, I want you to think about the most beautiful song you've ever heard. One that's so beautiful that it gives you goose bumps, maybe even makes you tear up. Maybe something by Mozart. Or Bach. Or Celine Dion. Leonard Cohen, perhaps. Maybe Louis Armstrong singing "What a Wonderful World." Don't spend too much time on it. Just pick one. Got it? Well, the aesthetic argument says that because that song exists, God must exist. And the same can be said for all the arts, as well as all the beautiful things in the natural world—sunsets, waterfalls, starry nights.

Not surprisingly, many have argued against this idea. Joseph McCabe (1867–1955) was a freethinker, meaning that he held the philosophical viewpoint that a person ought to form their own thoughts, as opposed to getting them from dogma or authority, and McCabe rightly noted that not everything created is beautiful. In his book *The Existence of God*, he contrasts a rose with a parasitic microbe and suggests that if one believes God created the first, they also have to believe God created the second. Richard Dawkins (b. 1941), British evolutionary biologist, emeritus fellow at Oxford, and famous atheist, will tell you that a beautiful Mozart piece proves not that God exists but that Mozart did. There's an inescapable logic to this, it seems to me.

But another Oxford Richard, Richard Swinburne (b. 1934)—emeritus professor of philosophy at Oxford, and famous theist[7] —wonders why the universe evolved to produce anything beautiful (like roses) when it could just as easily have produced nothing but ugliness (parasitic microbes *everywhere*). But he doesn't just mean the subjective appeal of a sunset. He also means the orderliness of the universe. The fact that it makes sense. The fact (to paraphrase) that atoms on Earth act the same as atoms on Mars. He makes a good point, too, I think. At least in my view, orderliness is a kind of beauty. The fact that two plus two equals four *every single time* is not to be underestimated in its elegance.

This idea comes close to the argument from design, but it goes a little deeper. It would be easy to say that the beauty of, say, a sunset

---

7. You can find an interesting dialogue between Dawkins and Swinburne on YouTube.

is a subjective thing. Some people might find sunsets hideous.[8] Music is subjective. You can go to YouTube right now and find a video of Leonard Bernstein conducting a symphony orchestra flawlessly performing Beethoven's Ninth Symphony ("Ode to Joy"), and you will find people who gave it a thumbs down![9] Thus demonstrating the subjectivity of beauty. (Conversely, some people probably find parasitic microbes beautiful.) But to contemplate concepts like math or physical laws, to consider their constancy and truth—these are not subjective.

Or are they? Would two plus two equal four if human beings did not exist? Or is two plus two a human construct? The question is not an idle one. What we're talking about here are what philosophers call *universals*, and philosophers have argued about them since Plato. Do scientific laws exist independently of our minds? That is, do we *discover* scientific laws or *construct* them? Well, it would seem strictly from a common-sense perspective that something like, for instance, the theory of gravity exists independently of us. Or, more accurately, gravity itself. Things would still fall *down* if humans weren't around, wouldn't they?

Okay, but what about a concept like, say, blue? Does blue exist independently of our minds? That's a tougher one to answer. The word "blue" belongs to us. Webster's definition of blue is ours. But the *concept*. What about that?

Plato made a clever allegory once about a cave, in which he imagined a group of people chained with their backs to the entrance. All they could see of the world were shadows on the wall in front of them. Not knowing any better, they imagined the shadows to be

---

8. These people would be a certain ex-girlfriend of mine who, sadly, didn't have a romantic bone in her body.

9. Or at least you could back when YouTube used to display a "dislike" count.

reality. But reality was happening outside in the sunshine. Is this us? Do we experience mere representations of reality? Plato's idea of universals, which he called *forms*, was that these concepts exist, but they come to us filtered, so to speak, by our senses and our minds. But for us to sense them at all, they have to be there in the first place. And so blue exists as a form, a universal. There's some perfect form of blue that is here, whether we are or not.

So can we say the same for beauty? Not the beauty of a particular piece of artwork, a particular song, or a particular sunset but beauty as a concept? Plato would say yes. Beauty exists independently of the human mind. Earlier, we discussed morality and the possibility of *its* existence absent humankind. Is morality like beauty, too?

If so, is this a valid argument for God? Maybe. If beauty or morality are mere human inventions (only in our heads), then we don't need God to explain their presence. But if they're here anyway, then what? It's worth asking whether we've invented beauty or discovered it and, if the latter, what the ramifications of that are.

Here's something else to think about: whether beauty is a figment of our imaginations or a universal phenomenon present as a reality in the universe, why do we experience it at all? And now we come full circle back to the experience thing. But instead of wondering what, exactly, experience is, I'm now wondering something else. I'm wondering what purpose it serves. The fact is that there is no useful function for our ability to appreciate beauty. There is no evolutionary reason for it. Why is it here? That great philosopher Sherlock Holmes once beheld a rose and remarked to his trusty sidekick Watson, "Our highest assurance of the goodness of Providence seems to me to rest in the flowers. All other things...are all really necessary for our existence. But this rose is an extra." You see, humans have never needed to appreciate beauty to survive. As far as we know, no other animal sits and gawks at a sunset. It's not a necessary element of life. Was it perhaps a gift?

Well, there are theories about this, as you may guess, that have nothing to do with gifts from God. Beauty came into our imaginations as some sort of byproduct of adaptation, a kind of accidental leaning toward the aesthetic at some point in our distant past. Maybe it's an offshoot of how we evolved to find certain people "attractive" so as to have sex with them and advance the species. And then this "attractive" idea sort of leaked into other areas of our lives, and we began to take pleasure in looking at certain sights or listening to certain sounds. Or maybe it was just a totally random thing.

Who knows, right?

Well, of course, that's the dilemma. If you'll recall from the first chapter, we can't *know*. Either way. Not 100 percent. But after finally navigating our way through the "Big Ten" of arguments for the existence of God,[10] maybe there are at least a few semi-conclusions we can draw. I say the time has come for us to pull all this stuff together and see if there's anything at all worth hanging on to. If you're up for it, let's do that in the next chapter.

---

10. Congrats for coming this far.

Chapter Six

A Preponderance, Perhaps?

A summary. The ontological argument—God exists because the greatest being that can be imagined would, of course, exist—is interesting, but I don't think persuasive. The cosmological argument—God as the first cause—is a popular argument for good reason. It sure explains a lot, like, you know, the origin of the universe, something no other theory has definitively explained. The teleological argument or argument from design explains a lot, too, like how our universe was set up perfectly to produce sentient life.

The historical argument depends on texts that are ancient and unverifiable, yet the argument is fascinating all the same. The moral argument asks where altruism came from if not from God, and science's answer of evolution is far from conclusive. The existential argument and Pascal's wager give us pragmatic reasons to believe, suggesting that it's in our best interest to do so.

The prevalence of religious experience is enough to make a person wonder just what the heck is going on here, anyway. Experience itself leads to the argument of mind–body dualism, an assertion that there is more to the universe than the physical world. And this possibility suggests the aesthetic argument, which is that there's real beauty present that we *discover* rather than develop or invent. Furthermore, our experience of these aesthetic properties seems to serve no necessary, evolutionary purpose.

See anything you like?

There are a few of these that I think are worth revisiting, starting with the cosmological argument. Frankly, the idea of a universe that is "neither created nor destroyed" (in Stephen Hawking's words) gives me a headache. The closed-loop theory is just that—a theory. And in thinking about theories that postulate a universe without a starting point, we end up mired in the confusing Swamp of Infinity, land of weird paradoxes. Many big brains have pointed out the strange characteristics of infinity, the way we use it like a number to describe an amount, and yet it doesn't at all behave like a number. If I subtract from infinity, I still get infinity. Infinity minus thirty equals infinity. But isn't it thirty less? Nope. If I add to infinity, I get... more infinity?

There's a famous thought experiment called "Hilbert's Hotel," introduced by influential German mathematician David Hilbert (1862–1943). He asks us to think about a "grand hotel" with an infinite number of rooms. All of them happen to be occupied. The hotel is full! Nevertheless, if you go to the front desk, they'll be able to find you a room because, well, they have an infinite number of them. Of course, they can't give you the last room in the place because there isn't a "last" one, so you'd never get there. But they can give you the first one, meaning they can just usher you into Room 1 and tell everybody to move one room over. Room 2 moves to Room 3, Room 3 moves to Room 4, Room 4 moves to Room 5, and so on. Of course, the moving would never end, but at least you'd have your room for the night. Now, what if an infinite number of guests all showed up at the same time looking for rooms? Well, if the desk clerk was smart, rather than moving everybody infinitely from room to room, he might try to solve the problem by moving everybody currently in the hotel to even-numbered rooms and all the new people into odd-numbered rooms.[1] Now you have two sets of rooms. But you see what has happened? The clerk has effectively divided the hotel in half, but *each half is just as big as the original.* Two subsets of an infinite set are themselves infinite. How's a guy supposed to make sense of something like this? The concept is absurd.

If it doesn't make intuitive sense, it's because you're probably used to dealing with finite numbers. And why wouldn't you be? Infinity is nothing more than an abstract concept. We have nothing equivalent to Hilbert's Hotel in the real world. There is nothing in the physical world that is infinite. Nothing. (With the possible exception of the universe itself; we just don't know.)

Any first-year philosophy student is familiar with the concept of *Occam's razor*. William of Occam (1287–1347), a famous medieval philosopher, basically said that when considering two competing ideas, it's generally a good idea to pick the one with fewer assumptions. The simpler idea, other things held equal, is more likely to be true. Shave away the more complex one. Now, this is more of a rule of thumb than anything else. Nobody can claim that Occam's razor is foolproof, and I imagine that a smarter fellow than myself might be able to use Occam's razor to dispel Occam's razor. Nonetheless, this whole infinity thing might be a good place to use it. A beginning point complete with a first cause just makes a hell of a lot more *sense* than the bizarre theoretical attributes of circular, infinite time. That doesn't make it true, of course. It made sense for *Saving Private Ryan* to win Best Picture at the Academy Awards in 1999. But that didn't happen. *Shakespeare in Love* won. *Shakespeare in Love.* Over *Saving Private Ryan.* (!) So "sense" isn't

---

1. Imagine the infinite number of bad Yelp reviews!

always a given.[2] The point is that a theory that doesn't involve an infinite set of events is a simpler theory, and pulling out Occam's razor might be entirely appropriate here.

On the other hand, a finite universe doesn't settle things. A first cause tells us nothing about the nature of the cause. It doesn't tell us that the cause was God. Maybe something else happened in that time*less* Big Bang "moment" when the laws of physics were only rumors. And so the cosmological argument is not a very complete one. But maybe it's better than invoking a concept (infinity) that is *only* conceptual or a theory (the Big Bang) that relies on a breakdown of everything we know.

Ironically, being "merely theoretical" is a charge often leveled by atheists about belief in God. Face it: we all pick our theories.

So which is the best? Well, to consider believing in God, it might help if we knew more about God, apart from the speculation that he was the guy who flipped on the switch for the universe. Does God as designer help? I struggle with the idea of life spontaneously arising from lifeless matter. Maybe it makes perfect sense to you, but it strikes me as unlikely. I know that earlier, I quoted geologist Cesare Emiliani, who not only believed that the appearance of life was likely but "a foregone conclusion." Others aren't so sure, however. As it happens, we now know that life, particularly the replication of life, requires more than just a "primordial soup" of chemicals. It requires *information*. And that information is encoded in DNA. Deoxyribonucleic acid is a polymer that basically acts as the playbook for the functioning, growth, and reproduc-

---

2. Rumor has it that the producer of *Shakespeare in Love* went all in on an intense, rampaging press campaign for his film, a campaign both excessive and shameless. (But obviously successful.) That producer happened to be an excessive and shameless guy by the name of Harvey Weinstein.

tion of every organism. You simply can't have life without it. And so if you propose that life spontaneously came about from dead matter, you have to explain a classic chicken-and-egg quandary. How did life come about without the necessary information for life (DNA), and how did the necessary information come about without life?

Well, there is a theory.[3] The RNA world hypothesis postulates that ribonucleic acid (RNA), a kind of less sophisticated polymer than DNA that is still able to carry and replicate genetic information, came along first, giving us an RNA world that, through evolutionary processes, ultimately gave way to today's DNA world. But this hypothesis presents problems, too. No matter how much simpler RNA is, it's still incredibly complex and, for all intents and purposes, impossible to imagine forming on its own. Even some proponents of the RNA world hypothesis agree. Gerald Joyce, chief science officer at the Salk Institute for Biological Studies, has written that "the problem of the origin of the RNA world is far from being solved, and it is fruitful to consider the alternative possibility that RNA was preceded by some other replicating, evolving molecule, just as DNA and proteins were preceded by RNA." So now we have to do more reverse engineering and postulate another step to explain how the chicken came before the egg. We need yet another theory. It's not very good, but for now, the RNA world hypothesis is the best one going. Harold Bernhardt, Research Fellow at the Department of Biochemistry at the University of Otago in New Zealand, calls it the *worst* theory of the early evolution of life, "except for all the others."

Of course, you could always fall back on the infinite universes theory. No matter how impossible it is for RNA to form, if

---

3. There's always a theory.

you had an infinite number of monkeys checking into a hotel, wait—there's the phone. Hey, it's William of Occam calling!

Remember famed atheist Antony Flew? I mentioned him when we originally discussed the design argument. He wondered why God wouldn't just snap his omnipotent fingers to produce life. Well, perhaps, in some sense, God did just this. Interestingly, Antony Flew himself eventually came around to this conclusion. Toward the end of his life, he became a deist, a believer, that is to say, in some creative force that can help explain the above conundrum, which he acknowledged was a stumper. It's important to note that Flew never (so far as anyone knows) became a believer in, say, the Christian God, but he nevertheless came to believe in a creator god.

If it's difficult to imagine life randomly springing forth from dead matter, it's just as difficult to imagine consciousness springing forth from life. And here, I'd like to return us to the hard problem of consciousness. David Chalmers, who first introduced the term "hard problem," talks about zombies. Not the brain-eating kind from the movies. Chalmers, rather, talks about zombies that look and act just like us. The only difference between us and these zombies is that while we are conscious, they aren't. If you prick them with a needle, they say, "Hey! Cut it out!" And if you ask, "Are you conscious?" they'd say, "Of course I am!" But in reality, these zombies aren't conscious at all—they're empty shells that act just like us but without experiencing. Got it? Okay, well, the punchline of this zombie argument is this: if zombies are possible, then it's possible that creatures could have the *exact same* brain events as you and me and yet not be conscious. And if that's true, then there must be consciousness, because we have it, and they don't. Now, there have been a lot of really dry arguments over the usefulness of all this zombie talk, but Chalmers's larger point still stands. He's illustrating, you see, what's become known as "the explanatory gap" between the strictly physical world and the conscious one: we can have all the same material processes and brain events as we do in our world, and yet the world could be devoid of consciousness (a zombie world). This tells us that you need to add an ingredient to get consciousness. Something—let us say God—has to sprinkle experience onto the world.

Now, besides conceding that there's a non-physical realm to the universe, one can try bridging this explanatory gap by denying consciousness or even denying the self, à la Daniel Dennett. These things simply don't exist except in the abstract. We are nothing more than neurons firing and chemical processes in our brains, holding onto the fiction of a self that is, in reality, nothing more than a bundle of related experiences. We are, well, not much different from zombies. But zombies who *think* they're having experiences because they don't realize that they aren't really conscious selves.

Which means we don't *really* experience beauty, even if we think we do. (Richard Swinburne makes a good point here. He says that if you're deluded into thinking you're having an experience, that in itself is an experience!) I'd like to add another experience to the aesthetic argument, since it seems we've now segued into it: *love*. Here's a thought experiment that involves neither hotels nor zombies. Think about the person you are closest to in this world. The person with whom you experience your most loving relationship. Maybe it's your significant other. Maybe it's a son or daughter or your children collectively. Maybe it's a parent. Or a best friend. (If you're a sociopath and you can't feel love, you're free to skip ahead.) If one doesn't believe in anything that transcends the material world, then one believes that such an experience—the experience of love, perhaps a very deep, significant experience—is really nothing more than neurons firing in the brain and that it exists only within the confines of one's skull, *separate and apart* from anybody else's reality. You're not really connecting with this other person I asked you to think about; it only seems like it. But there is no connection, not a literal one, anyway.

This is the only way love can be if it's the result strictly of evolution.

The other choice is to believe that you and the person you love so much are tapping into something larger than yourselves. Something outside of both of you. Something important and meaningful, something here for us to discover, and not the imaginative workings of a brain that has convinced its owner that it is a real self and not a deluded zombie. In a very real way, you and this other person *connect*.

Neither possibility is provable, but *if* reality is represented by the latter, then we owe it to ourselves to consider the true source of love. The same as we have to consider the true source of beauty (the appreciation of which, you'll recall, has no definite evolutionary reason for being). The same way we have to consider the true source of morality, especially in light of the evolutionary problem of altruism.

The experience of love, in fact, is described by many theologians as a religious experience. Often quoted is 1 John 4:16: "God is love, and he who abides in love abides in God and God in him." After all, if love exists independent of us, then by definition, the experience of it is a transcendent one. By this thinking, you may have had a religious experience and not even known it! Your love for that special person in your life is a religious experience, and you can now join the fifty percent of the population that claims to have had such an experience.

Or else it's all a bunch of hooey. That's definitely a possibility.

I think it's important to acknowledge that no argument we've discussed is enough to swing anybody over to the "more reasonable than not" standard we introduced at the very start of this book. Certainly not in my estimation, and probably not in yours. No argument *on its own*, that is. But the legal profession has a standard called "the preponderance of the evidence." Maybe we can make use of it.

The collective facts are roughly these: absent the concept of God, we don't have an adequate explanation for the beginning of the universe. We don't have an adequate explanation for how life evolved from dead matter. We don't have an adequate explanation for why we experience things. We don't have an adequate explanation for why we appreciate beauty. We don't have an adequate explanation for sacrifice. We don't have an adequate explanation for why love feels so damn significant to us when it's only in our heads. And we don't have an adequate explanation for the massive prevalence of religious experience.

Now, "adequate" is a subjective word. Every single one of these charges can be countered! I'm not going to pretend they can't be. Time could be infinite, regardless of how absurd the concept of infinity appears. Physical laws break down at the singularity. There was some rudimentary step before RNA that, no matter how impossible, nevertheless arrived on the scene and got the evolutionary ball rolling. Experience assumes a consciousness that either doesn't exist or is the result of something created by the brain that we simply don't understand. Aesthetic appreciation came about from evolution, just like sacrifice did, even if we can't say how. Sure, love is just in our heads, but so what? It still feels good. Morality is in our heads, too, just like the color blue. And 165 million Americans, otherwise well-meaning (most of them), are out of their heads with mass hysteria.

It is not for me to declare for you which set of beliefs is likelier to be true. You have your own standard. I'm just a guide, remember? I would only suggest (as your humble servant) that it appears as though theism explains things better than atheism. Does it comprehensively explain everything? Well, maybe not, but it seems to do the most with the least, and at some point, it might be worth considering Occam's razor to address all these points with the simplest explanation of all: there is a God. Boom. Everything gets wrapped up in a nice, tidy little package.

Or not. It's up to you. You might think that the idea of God's existence does nothing more than quell our human confusion over some of the more perplexing issues I've raised. A *God of the gaps*, as it's been popularly termed, hardly makes such a God real. We need more than belief based on a convenient explanation. Nevertheless, given the preponderance of perplexity, it seems, at least in my view, almost unnecessarily stubborn to cling to the position that God must not exist. Even if you dismiss any three or four of the above-referenced points, you have to admit you still have some 'splainin' to do on the others. "Damn it," you'd have to be saying, red-faced and in obstinate defiance. "I will *not* believe! And nobody can make me! No matter what!"

Is that you? Well, okay. That's your right. Besides, I think I know what's really eating you. Invoking the idea of a God, even if such a God legitimately fills the gaps, is not without its problems. In fact, bringing God into one's worldview can create a lot more questions than answers, and perhaps you are right to still be questioning. If God exists, there are some confusing issues about life that have to be addressed. We've discussed the pro arguments. Now, let's discuss the con.

CHAPTER SEVEN

THE BIG UGLY SIX

Interestingly, the term "God of the gaps" was first articulated not by an atheist, as one might imagine, but by a theist. It was still meant pejoratively, however. Henry Drummond (1851–1897), Scottish evangelist and biologist,[1] didn't care for the way that Christians proclaimed God's existence by explaining the unknown with his (God's) name, using God to fill in the gaps of our knowledge. God was more than this, Drummond felt. God is "infinitely grander than the occasional wonderworker."

Frankly, I don't care for this "gap" use of God by theists, either. There's got to be more, which is to say that I believe more is needed than the plethora of unexplained phenomena I listed in the last chapter, no matter how intimidating, even overwhelming, and certainly head-scratching that list might be.[2] Especially if we're going to address all the objections you still have. And that means this is a good time to consider the arguments that have been presented over the centuries for the proposition that God does *not* exist. Yours is probably in here somewhere:

---

1. And yet another smart guy with more than one career.

2. Or how simple it would be to solve the perplexities by simply saying, "God."

- The argument of theological noncognitivism

- The argument from divine hiddenness

- The argument that science explains everything (or will)

- The problem of evil

- The contradictions of religion

- The argument of incompatible properties

Let's call these the "Big Six." Okay, so it's not ten, but don't be discouraged. Quality is much more important than quantity. (Besides, you'll find that Number Six on the list comes with several little sub-arguments.) Just like the "pro" list, this list doesn't represent every argument that's ever been made but focuses on the more famous and best articulated ones.

Theological noncognitivism is a fancy-schmancy way of saying that the concept of God just doesn't make sense *linguistically*. This argument asks, What does the word "God" even *mean*, anyway? Who can define it? It's too unintelligible to be discussed in any reasonable way, so why are we talking about it in the first place? Forget it already. And if the term "God" is too ambiguous to meaningfully chat about, then the phrase "God exists" is even more so. End of story. Nothing more to see here, folks.

Philosopher and atheist George H. Smith (1949–2022) made the further point that even fictional items can be defined, so long as we understand their attributes, but God can't be defined because God has no meaningful attributes. "We may define the essence of a unicorn," Smith says, "without implying that unicorns actually exist." We all understand the concept of a horse-like thing with a big horn. Unicorns, therefore, actually have more meaning than God. So God is not only fictional but meaningless to boot.

Now, if this is your particular stand, I might argue that you're not a true atheist, for an atheist will tell you that they do not believe in "God." What sense can that make if the theist's claim that "God exists" is considered nonsensical? A theological noncognitivist must, by their own logic, be an agnostic, not an atheist. The moment you invoke the term "God," I'm going to assume that you have a concept in mind, some collective attributes, thus invalidating your argument that *God* is a conceptual non-starter.

But even from an agnostic standpoint, I find this argument weak and I do so by appealing to common sense. I suspect that people who hold this view do, in fact, have a concept in their heads. I mean, you and I know what we're talking about, right? Creator of the universe? Supreme Being? Big Cheese? Come on, stop being obtuse.

Now, it's true that there are many and varied concepts of God. Vishnu is different from Yahweh who is different from Allah. A deist believes in a much different kind of God than a pantheist. Point granted. So perhaps we need a definition. For now, let me just say this: this book, as it continues to unfold, is going to present a conception of God. A specific theory. Hopefully, by the time we're finished, you'll at least know what *I* mean by the term. If you still find it too fuzzy and senseless to be taken seriously, that would be a good time to play the theological noncognitivism card. Toss it onto the table and holler, "Payne, you're babbling! You're completely incomprehensible! Put the bottle down and go to bed!"[3] Hang on to that card until then. In the meantime, let's move forward with

---

3. You would not be the first.

some arguments that I, perhaps presumptuously, believe suit your position much better.

The argument from divine hiddenness asks a simple question: If God exists, how come we never see him? Even the people who claim to have had some kind of transcendent religious experience rarely talk about actually seeing God. Maybe they sense a presence, maybe they even hear a voice, but you never hear of someone sitting at a Denny's with God or playing a round of golf with him. This, by the way, has been a problem for theists through the ages, back through biblical times. David cries out in Psalm 22, "My God, my God, why has thou forsaken me? Why art thou so far from helping me?" On the cross, Jesus repeated, "My God, my God, why has thou forsaken me?"

In fact, more than one scholar has pointed out[4] that, although God is very present and accessible toward the front of the Hebrew Bible—revealing himself to Adam and Eve, Noah, Moses—he completely disappears by the end. And theists have struggled with this hiddenness ever since. Saint Anselm of Canterbury (1033–1109) wrote, "I have never seen thee, O Lord my God; I do not know thy form. What, O most high Lord, shall this man do, an exile far from thee?" Saint John of the Cross (1542–1591) referred to this painful absence as his "Dark Night of the Soul."[5]

---

4. Probably none more eloquently than Richard Elliott Friedman in his 1995 book *The Disappearance of God: A Divine Mystery* (Little, Brown and Company).

5. St. John of the Cross's "Dark Night of the Soul" was described in his poem "Dark Night" (*Noche Oscura*) written about 1579. He later wrote a commentary on the poem, also called "Dark Night." Want to hear a beautiful song? Listen to Loreena McKennit's "Dark Night of the Soul." She uses John's lyrics and, wow, is it a masterpiece or what?

It hasn't gotten any better since. God just doesn't seem to be around. And it's the same with people of every faith. Serious reports of God's appearance are nonexistent. I'm surprised his picture hasn't shown up on a milk carton. Why is this?

Although people have been asking questions about God's disappearance for centuries, the argument from divine hiddenness has more recently been popularized by Canadian philosopher John L. Schellenberg (b. 1959) in his influential book *Divine Hiddenness and Human Reason*. Schellenberg talks of wannabe believers who nevertheless just don't believe. Maybe you know someone like this. Someone who's not necessarily opposed to being a theist but can't bring themselves to believe that God exists. God wouldn't allow there to be such people, right? He'd always make sure that anyone who wasn't opposed to having a relationship with him would, at the very least, come to know that he's real. But God doesn't seem to do this, argues Schellenberg. Ipso facto, God does not exist. If he did, wouldn't everyone be a believer?

Make no mistake. This is a damn fine argument. Theists often counter with half-baked rebuttals like, "Well, God wants you to believe based on faith." Faith is apparently more important than fact. "Blessed are those who have not seen, and have believed," says Jesus in the book of John. But why? To Schellenberg's point, if God was a loving God, wouldn't he want to make sure we knew about him, especially those who were open to him? Remaining hidden is poor marketing. Letting people know you're around is why Budweiser spent $100 million on advertising last year. $100 million! And everybody already agrees that Budweiser exists. How much did God spend?

Of course, another half-baked rebuttal is what we covered earlier. God has revealed himself in the biblical record. In the holy texts. But we decided this was a weak argument, didn't we? I'm pretty sure we did. It was a while ago, and I'm too lazy to go back and check, but I don't remember thinking I convinced you of God's existence based on the holy books of the world's great religions.

Christians believe that God did, in fact, appear in the person of Christ. Jesus was God incarnate. But even if this were true, why did he leave, and why has he not come back? He will, Christians say. The Second Coming is nigh. Says every generation since Jesus's own.

Look, I know that I'm in a tight spot on this one. If God exists, the puzzle of his having gone AWOL is going to have to be solved. Duly noted.

In the meantime, let's address *the argument that science explains everything (or will)*. This is a really common argument, but it's not one you should be hanging your hat on. We know from our discussion so far that science has quite a bit it has yet to explain. Will it one day uncover the secrets to the origin of the universe? Will it be able to someday tell us how sentient life evolved from dead matter? Will science solve the hard problem of consciousness or perhaps confirm that the self is an illusion?

Maybe. But here's the thing: if there is more to the universe than the natural world, science will never be able to help us because everything beyond the natural world is out of science's purview. There is the natural world, and there is (perhaps) the spiritual world. Science can only deal with the former, but that doesn't negate the possibility of the latter, which doesn't play by the rules of science and can therefore go unrecognized by it. This might explain that Pew survey from earlier that revealed that 51 percent of scientists believe in God. Science can't prove God, but science can't disprove God, either. This, after all, is why we've gone the route of the philosophers with this book. The philosophers are the ones suited to exploring the questions of God, not the scientists.

Scientists understand this. Listen to big-brained quantum physicist Erwin Schrödinger (1887–1961), he of "Schrödinger's cat" fame: "I am very astonished that the scientific picture of the real world around me is very deficient. It gives us a lot of factual information and puts all of our experience in a magnificently consistent order, but it is ghastly silent about all and sundry that is really near to our heart that really matters to us. It knows nothing of beautiful and ugly, good and bad, God and eternity."

And it's not just that these sorts of concepts are outside of science's domain. It's also a question of gaining the proper perspective to study them objectively. Nobel-Prize-winning physicist Max Planck (1858–1947), considered the father of quantum physics, put it like this in his classic *Where is Science Going?*: "Science cannot solve the ultimate mystery of nature. And that is because, in the last analysis, we ourselves are part of nature and therefore part of the mystery that we are trying to solve." Think about studying consciousness, for instance—as conscious beings, using our consciousness, the very thing we are trying to study. See the problem? We're on the inside trying to study an external (objective) reality.

And think about this for a second: science assumes there is an objective reality to study, but what is this assumption based on, since we can't get outside of it? Good question. Planck had the only answer: "Over the entrance to the gates of the temple of science are written the words: *Ye must have faith*." See what he did there? He said something very similar to what Augustine believed. Faith precedes reason. Even in science. Interesting, no? I hereby deem the argument that science explains everything (or will) a big swing and a miss. And I would ask it to take a seat in favor of the next argument.

The problem of evil is the equivalent of the theistic cosmological argument in that it would probably win an atheistic argument popularity contest, hoisted onto shoulders and paraded around. Admit it: this is the one you've been waiting for. I put it fourth in the lineup because that's where you put the big clean-up hitter. It's the go-to argument.

It runs like this: *God exists? Really? Then how do you explain all the evil in the world? Hmm? Well?*

There is a remarkable little book called *Night*, written by Nobel-prize winner Elie Wiesel. It's the moving, dramatic recounting of his time as a teenager in the Auschwitz and Buchenwald concentration camps during the Holocaust. He sees his family die around him. He sees his faith die. At one point, he relates the story of a child being hanged by the guards in view of the other prisoners, who watch as the child slowly suffocates and dies. From behind him, Wiesel hears a man say, "For God's sake, where is God?" Wiesel writes, "And from within me, I heard a voice answer: 'Where He is? This is where—hanging here from this gallows.'"

God was dead to Wiesel at that point, or at least dying. And who wouldn't think the same, no matter how pious and faithful? Interestingly, in a 2003 interview, Wiesel spoke of his faith. It never really died. "I never divorced God," he said. "It is because I believed in God that I was angry at God, and still am. The tragedy of the believer, it is deeper than the tragedy of the non-believer."

You see, this problem of evil is a bigger problem for theists than for atheists. An atheist can point to the Holocaust, declare that God obviously doesn't exist, and then go about their life. Theists have to find a way to reconcile how God and something as evil as the Holocaust can co-exist. We can't just get on with our lives.

So what do we theists tell ourselves? Why is there evil?

Well, one explanation is philosophical simplicity itself. Evil exists because good exists, just as dark exists because light exists, or cold exists because warmth exists. Once you bring one into the world, you've got the other—the counterpart. Philosophers call this "counterpart theodicy." Personally, I'm not sold on it. For one thing, it doesn't explain the degree of evil in the world. Also, it's not entirely clear to me that counterparts have to exist. Who says so?

But right now, I've got a more fundamental question for you. If we're going to use these terms—"good" and "evil"—then I've got to wonder what we mean by them. Aren't they subjective? You can find people in the world right now (and certainly at the time of its implementation, i.e., the Nazis) who would tell you that the Holocaust was a good thing. How are we to argue against them? Well, we could say that genocide is evil. Mass killings are wrong. Massacring innocents is bad. But do we have an objective, absolute standard that we can rely on to confirm these statements? An atheist must deny that such a thing exists. An absolute standard brings us back to the universals idea from earlier. If you agree that there is an objective, absolute morality, I'm going to have to ask you about its source. And what could your answer be? This was the argument of Saint Aquinas, Kant, and C. S. Lewis, if you'll recall.

It's not enough if even 99,999 out of 100,000 people say the Holocaust was evil. Without an absolute standard to appeal to, it's still a subjective thing, making the word "evil" itself meaningless, outside of purely pragmatic usage. Evil is whatever we decide we don't like. If you say that evil exists, then you're implying a universal, absolute standard. And an absolute standard implies God. In this way, the existence of evil, suggesting as it does an objective morality, is an argument better made *for* God's existence than against it.

How about that for some philosophical jujitsu? Now, you could always concede that there's no objective morality and that, sure, "evil" is a term that might be up for grabs, but so what? After all, I just mentioned the word "pragmatic," so why not define "good" and "evil" in *useful* ways?

We said at the beginning of the book that we can't know anything with absolute certainty, so why am I even bringing absolutes into the discussion? Good point. Okay, I won't speak of absolutes. But I'm duty bound (as your trusty guide) to point out that you can't, either. Without a God, the Holocaust is evil by virtue of your opinion and nothing more. Now, you might share that opinion with most of humanity, but it's still an opinion.

But I think your real issue goes a little deeper, anyway. I suspect your problem isn't so much that evil exists, but more specifically why, if God exists, is evil allowed? Right? Isn't that your real question? And not just evil perpetrated by Nazis and sickos like, for instance, the Jeffrey Dahmer and Ted Bundy types, but what about all the bad things that happen naturally on this planet? Tornadoes and hurricanes and floods and mud slides and earthquakes and tsunamis and fires? What about those? What about disease? Pandemics? Childhood cancer? Why does God *allow* such things?

If there's a God, why does he allow *any* really bad thing to happen?

Well, I'm going to ask that you pocket that question for now. That's a question that has more to do with God's nature than God's existence. We're not there yet. But we'll get there. Just hang on. Your patience is appreciated, and you will be adequately rewarded. (Maybe.) While you're waiting, might I interest you in a lively discussion about the many contradictions of the world's religions?

The contradictions-of-religion argument is another very popular one, and for good reason. It is alternatively known as "the argument of inconsistent revelations" or—a favorite description of mine—"the avoiding-the-wrong-Hell problem." It's a bit like the theological noncognitivism argument in that it deals with God definitionally. But instead of dealing with God's ambiguity, this argument is pointed at specific definitions of God—or, more precisely, the huge number of definitions that exist. We alluded to this when we talked about Pascal's wager. It's one thing to bet on God if there's one distinct, agreed-upon concept of God. You've got yourself a fifty/fifty proposition. God or no God. But if your bet is between no God, the Christian God, or, say, Vishnu, your odds are now only one in three.

Note that this isn't a true argument against the existence of God. It could be that there is, in fact, one true conception of an existing God and that all other conceptions and attending revelations thereof are false. But the argument does make a good point. There are, in fact, some 4,200 religions in the world, and each has a different conception of the supreme being (although some of the differences are slight). Taking Pascal's wager gives you one chance in 4,201. Even less when you consider that some of the conceptions involve multiple gods.

These are not good odds.

Historian–philosopher and atheist Stephen F. Roberts (1958–2022), when addressing a theist, was fond of saying, "I contend we're both atheists. I just believe in one fewer god than you." Author, intellectual, and atheist Christopher Hitchens (1949–2011) was fond of repeating this, and I've heard other atheists use this argument, too. And why not? On the surface, it's a good one. Most people are indeed atheists when it comes to the other guy's god. On the other hand, *one* can make a huge difference in some cases. If I turned to my married friend Jarvis and said, "I contend we're both single; I just have one fewer wife than you," he'd wonder what I'd been smoking (and, knowing Jarvis, ask where he could get some).

But there's no denying that the Christian God is different from the Muslim God is different from the Hebrew God is different from the Hindu gods. Buddhists and Taoists, meanwhile, have a whole different take on the universe. Each religion has its sacred texts, as we discussed earlier in the book. And these are just the so-called major religions. Even within Christianity, there are different denominations. How many? Would you believe *45,000?* I didn't, either, but this is a number reported by the Center for the Study of Global Christianity, and who am I to argue?

A lot of these denominations have beliefs that are in contradiction with each other, which, of course, is why they split off in the first place. Most Protestant religions, for instance, believe that church doctrine can be found only in the Bible, whereas Catholics believe that doctrine can also come from popes and bishops. Christian Scientists don't believe in the holy trinity. Baptists don't believe in infant baptism, maintaining that the sacrament is only for someone mature enough to make a decision to be baptized. Some Churches of Christ don't believe in using musical instruments during worship services. And believe me, there are some strange denominations out there. Two words: *snake handling.* There's a slew of churches throughout the southern United States that practice this... um... unique ritual. Their definition of God *has* to be different from everybody else's, right?

But here's the problem I see with the contradictions-of-religion argument: it assumes we have to choose. And if we pick one, then we're necessarily rejecting the rest. Pascal is spinning his wheel, and we're supposed to throw our chips down on whatever god seems best to us and hope we're choosing correctly. Well, sure, that's problematic. But what if God's essence is something more along the lines of how Walt Whitman described himself in his classic poem "Song of Myself" where he asks, "Do I contradict myself?; Very well then I contradict myself; I am large, I contain multitudes." Maybe God isn't any one definition. Maybe God, to some degree, is all of them, each one the natural result of humans flailing about in human language and in human ritual, reaching the upper limits of their imaginations to try to describe this ineffable thing we refer to as "God." So rather than saying I do not believe in 4,199 gods, it just might be more accurate for me to say that I believe, in some respects, in all of them all rolled into one. God contains multitudes.

Now, I know what you're thinking. You're thinking I'm quite mad. More to the point, you're thinking I've fallen into a theological noncognitivism trap. (Good for you; it shows you've been paying attention.) A god that encompasses 4,200 definitions is a god without any definition at all. When we define something, we identify its essential meaning or qualities. We consider that which makes it distinct. If we open up the tent to 4,200 different interpretations, have we accomplished anything meaningful? What sense can such a god make? Defining God as basically indefinable is a paradox that I'm aware I'm going to need to deal with before the end of this book.

And there are more. *The argument of incompatible properties* presents us with several seemingly head-scratching contradictions and puzzles about God, many of which go back to the Greeks and have been debated for centuries. The problem of evil is such an important one of these contradictions that I classified it as a separate argument. How can a God worthy of worship allow bad things to happen? But there are other puzzling riddles, mainly having to do with the typical attributes ascribed to God. God is characterized as omniscient, unchanging, perfect, and all-powerful. But these attributes come with a few problems.

First, if God is omniscient, that must mean he knows even the future. So does this mean that the future is, in some sense, set in stone? What does this say about human free will? Is it nonexistent? Are we merely going through the motions of lives that are predetermined? What would be the purpose of such a creation?

And if God is unchanging, then how does one explain the temporal activity of creating the universe? This question was asked earlier and without an adequate answer (which, we decided, is a problem for both sides of the debate, unless you want to subscribe to the idea of an infinite universe).

But even if you can explain away the moment of creation, if God is perfect, then what is the need for anything more? What is the need for even creating a universe? And wouldn't the creation of a perfect being, if the being is indeed perfect, necessarily have to be perfect as well? How can a perfect being create imperfection? And yet it's pretty clear that humans are about as far from perfect as you can get. Just watch the news, why don't you. Or observe people departing a commercial airplane. Sheesh. How long does it take to grab a bag from the overhead compartment and head for the front exit already?

There's no escaping it; the concept of God is riddled with, well, riddles. The famous stone paradox is popular among atheists. Can an all-powerful God make a stone that is so heavy that he himself cannot lift it? If he can't, then he's not all powerful. But if he can, then he's also not all powerful because he can't lift the stone.

A theist could argue that what would really happen if God took on such a task is that he would create the heaviest rock of all time and then lift it. So then he'd create an even heavier rock, and, of course, he'd be able to lift that one, too. And then he'd create an even heavier rock to lift. And on and on. God would infinitely be creating rocks that he could lift, and so the paradox is actually a testament to God's infinite power, not an argument against it.

Probably a better way to respond to the paradox, however, is to invoke C. S. Lewis, who said of these types of paradoxes, "[God's] omnipotence includes power to do all that is intrinsically possible, not to do the intrinsically impossible. You may attribute miracles to Him, but not nonsense."

But some of these riddles produce serious questions. Like this headscratcher: If God is transcendent, then how can he participate in time? If God created the universe, then God created space and time, right? So that means God is outside of time. This presents serious problems for the theist who argues that God is omnipresent and somehow accessible. But how can a being who is outside of time possibly be a part of a temporal world? Now, we can summon Antony Flew's ultimate thoughts about God as creator only, the guy who flipped on the switch and walked away. This is what deists believe. But this is surely not a God worthy of veneration, and certainly not the God most religious people have in mind.

How are we to make sense of all these conundrums?

Well, I reckon I had better try. That's why you're still reading, I presume. Let's start talking less about God's existence and, as I've been promising, more about God's nature, with the latter hopefully answering some of your questions about the former.

Chapter Eight

Now, Here's an Interesting Worldview

So what do you think so far? Does the concept of God seem any more plausible, interesting, reasonable, or thought-provoking than it did when you started this book?

We've come a long way, after all. Two chapters ago, we created a laundry list of inexplicable characteristics of life and the universe. Well, there was one possible explanation: God. But in the last chapter, we detailed some objections. We reviewed the argument of theological noncognitivism, deciding that although the term "God" can be a nebulous one, it might be considered poor form to just up and leave the discussion on the grounds of nebulosity.[1] Especially since you've been assured that a less nebulous definition will eventually be forthcoming. Moreover, the argument flies in the face of common sense: Surely, we know what theists mean when they say, "God exists." Or at least, surely, atheists know what theists mean, because they typically respond by saying, "No, he doesn't."

We also discussed the argument from divine hiddenness, and the argument that science explains everything (or will). The for-

---

1. That's right, I used the word "nebulosity." It's not a real word, but I don't care and I won't apologize. (And, hey, you probably understood what I meant, anyway, right? Heh-heh.)

mer definitely needs to be addressed by yours truly, but the latter seems, frankly, a bit weak, especially since we know there is much that science has not explained and may never explain, given its less-than-objective position on the inside of the things it is trying to study.

The problem of evil was discussed and further refined to the question of "Why?" and I have promised that we'll get there. Then, we covered the contradictions-of-religion argument, where I submitted that the contradictions fall apart if you accept the definitions of *all* of the many religions of the world. But this, too, has its problems. Finally, we spent a little time on the argument of incompatible properties. There are paradoxes seemingly everywhere with this whole God idea.

In my estimation, this last objection is atheism's best and brightest, particularly the paradox we ended the chapter on. How can God, being creator of, and outside of, time, possibly be a part of our temporal world? If God is nothing more than the flipper of the switch, then for all intents and purposes, I don't find much difference between believing in God and being an atheist. Either way, we're still all alone in the cosmos, drifting along without any transcendent meaning or purpose.

If we can't find a way around this paradox, then I don't see how any of the arguments—pro or con—even matter. It's game over.

So, what do I have to say for myself on this critical, make-or-break issue? Wanting God to participate in time is more than wishful thinking. Frankly, it just doesn't make sense that God would create something off limits for him. For what purpose? God's creation must be accessible to God.

If you're having trouble imagining why God's participation in time presents a logical problem, try to picture God watching a video called *Life on Earth*. He created the video, so he's not in it.

He's outside of it, as creator and as observer. But it's all there in front of him. Since the video runs in chronological time, *which he is not subject to*, he can skip to anywhere he likes. Of course, the people in the video can't do this. They're stuck having to play out their parts in chronological time and cannot see further into the video than where they now are. So how does God participate in this video? How does he interact with the players? Even if he could somehow inject himself into *Life on Earth* to, say, make a change in the plot, what becomes of the first plot? Is it still there? Well, of course it is, because it already happened, or else he would not have seen it to make the change.

See how squirrely things get? And it's even more so when you consider that all the activities I just described God doing are temporal in nature. Creating, observing, skipping around, making changes—these require time, which God, as creator of time, is on the outside of. Bottom line: His participation in time is nonsensical.

How to get out of this conundrum? Well, maybe it would help if we better understood the concept of time. What is it, anyway? Does anybody really know what time it is? Does anybody really care? The band Chicago clearly didn't. But for our purposes, it might help if we could at least understand what *it is*.

Not surprisingly, the ancient Greeks had some ideas on the subject but were not in complete agreement. Aristotle believed that time is movement. Imagine everything in the room where you're sitting, including you, suddenly freezing in place. Nothing moves. Your heart is frozen between beats. Nothing moves outside, either. Or throughout the town or city where you live or even in the whole universe! Aristotle would tell you that time has thus ceased. But then something suddenly falls off your wall. A picture comes loose.

Boom. *Time*. See? Things need to happen. Time is occasions, events—temporal relationships between things and action.

Plato, on the other hand, believed that time is independent of events. Time is like a track on which things are placed. Or a tunnel through which things move. It's a measurable fourth dimension. There's height, depth, width, and time. And it's there whether things are frozen or not. Among the big-brained people, Gottfried Leibnitz and Immanuel Kant sided with Aristotle, with Sir Isaac Newton (1642–1727) notably carrying the mantle for Plato.

But a lot has happened since those guys. As the great philosopher Jeffrey Lebowski would say, new shit has come to light. What does modern science have to tell us about time? Well, Albert Einstein (1879–1975) threw a monkey wrench into the works the day he proved that everyone's common sense ideas about time were just plain wrong. Time, it turns out, is relative. Its rate of movement depends on one's frame of reference. Einstein essentially said that it wasn't enough to describe the location of an object by the standard three-dimensional coordinates. You need to describe where it is in time, too. Space and time are inextricably linked, and physicists now talk about spacetime. By so doing, science appears to favor time as a dimension, just as Plato believed. On the other hand, what is time without space (or matter)? Not much.

Whether one believes in time as the events of matter or time as a dimension, it seems clear that time exists because space exists. The universe is space. And the universe is time. The universe is composed of stuff—space, matter, planets, you and me. And it's all bound up with time.

What this means is that for God to act within time, God needs to be able to act within space. But now we still have the problem we had with time. How can God act within space if he created it and is on the outside looking in? There is an answer. At least a possibility.

God can act within space (and therefore time) because—get ready to have your mind blown—God *is* space. God is stuff—space, matter, planets, you and me. The time paradox is solved, you see, if you remove the premise that God is on the outside. Maybe God's not on the outside. Maybe God is on the inside. More precisely, maybe God *is* the inside.

How can one come to this conclusion? Well, you start with the idea that there's almost no other way out.[2] Let's you and I be honest. It's hard to get past that list of inexplicable characteristics about life and the universe from the end of Chapter 6 without invoking the concept of God, isn't it? But if God exists, it doesn't make sense that he'd create something he couldn't access. So, to reconcile this paradox, we really need to think outside of the philosophical box. And one way is to consider the idea that God is time and space.

There's another way. You can also do away with the time paradox if you—wait for it—do away with time! This is not as nutso as it sounds. There are a *lot* of big-brained folks who believe that time is an illusion. Think about it: Where is the past? Where is the future? Can you see either one? Can you even see the moment when you started reading this paragraph? Not remember it, but see it, experience it, feel it. Of course not. The moment is gone, and the moment when you start reading the next paragraph hasn't arrived yet. Every moment is like this. Remember the Buddhist idea of the no-self? It applies to time, too. We think of past and present and future as real things, but there's nothing real except the present moment, which, by the time you consider it, is already out of existence. What kind of reality is that?

---

2. And perhaps a six pack of beer.

John McTaggart Ellis McTaggart[3] (1866–1925), British meta-physician and lecturer at Trinity College in Cambridge, wrote a famous book in 1908 entitled *The Unreality of Time*. Philosophers still discuss it (and disagree over it). It's fairly detailed and complex, but McTaggart makes his titular point by arguing that concepts like *past*, *present*, and *future* are all contradictory and circular and, well, meaningless. McTaggart essentially said that for time to be real, the concepts of past, present, and future have to exist. But if an event is past, it cannot also be present. And yet, at some point, a past event *was* present. Every event contains a past, present, and future. Yet, past, present, and future are clearly incompatible properties. They contradict. See? Time just doesn't make sense. Hence, it doesn't exist.

McTaggart's position is not without controversy, but the idea of the past and future being basically hearsay (which has a certain intuitive sense about it, if you ask me) is interesting. If time *is* an illusion, perhaps even a human construct, then this solves a lot of problems, including the problem that creativity itself (i.e., the creation of the universe) is a temporal activity. If temporality is a mirage, then this problem goes away. Maybe there was no creative "moment." And, hey, guess what?—this would also explain the idea of a "perfect" being deciding to "add" to things by making up a universe. Nothing was added; it was already there. (McTaggart, interestingly, was an atheist. Of sorts. Oddly, he actually believed in souls, reincarnation, and immortality.)

---

3. This is not a misprint. He was born John McTaggart Ellis after his great uncle, Sir John McTaggart. Then, as a condition of inheritance from Great Uncle John, the family had to agree to take John McTaggart's last name. Hence, John McTaggart Ellis McTaggart. (Putting me in mind of Richard Heller's Major Major Major Major.)

In any event, to believe in a participatory God, a God that can act within time, one can believe either that God is time or that time does not exist. And if you're wondering how space can exist without time, well, there are quantum theories about that. Some physicists believe causation can exist without time, and causation can provide a sense that one thing can bring about another—a sense, that is to say, of events, which make up space. But this is all getting needlessly complicated. The thing to remember is this: God cannot act on that which is beyond God. For God to act in the world, the world must be within God. Part of God. Never created but always there, making sense of our existence with a relational tool that we call "time." A few paragraphs above, we talked about God being on the inside. Now, we're talking about us being on the inside of God. Both ideas are intriguing, and either way you arrive at it—God is time or time is an illusion—the idea of the universe being inextricably bound up with God, essentially making them one and the same, solves a few paradoxes.

And lest you think we're starting to swerve *way* out there (I see you out of the corner of my eye reaching for Occam's entire toolbelt), this idea has a grand philosophical tradition that I think is worth exploring, just to see where it takes us. Maybe nowhere. But I think we owe it to ourselves to learn a little bit about a worldview called *pantheism*.

From the Greek words *pan*, meaning "all," and *theos*, meaning "God," pantheism is the view that everything is God. But it wasn't the Greeks who used the word. It wasn't until 1697 that the word "pantheism" was minted by philosopher-mathematician Joseph Raphson (1668–1715) in describing a belief in "a certain universal substance, material as well as intelligent, that fashions all things that exist out of its own essence."

Nevertheless, Greek Stoicism, developed in the third century BCE, held a pantheistic point of view. God was not transcendent but always immanent. The Neoplatonists from around the third century CE believed in what came to be known as "emanationistic pantheism," a belief that everything flows from one reality, from God, as opposed to being created by God. And many very early religions, often with no central God figure, believed that the divine was everywhere and in everything—in nature, in animals, in the sky, in the earth.

Pantheism gained a little traction during the Middle Ages but started to become a dangerous view to hold as the power of the Catholic Church grew. Giordano Bruno (1548–1600) was a philosopher, mathematician, poet, and pantheist (although Raphson's word had yet to make an appearance). Bruno didn't believe a separation existed between God and his creation, and this was a dangerous belief at the time. In fact, in 1600, in the midst of the Roman Inquisition, Pope Clement VIII declared Bruno a heretic, and he was burned at the stake for his beliefs. But Bruno certainly had a pair. Here's what he said before they lit the match: "Perchance you who pronounce my sentence are in greater fear than I who receive it." How cool was that? (Definitely the coolest use of the word "perchance," that's for sure.)

Then along came Baruch Spinoza, whom we mentioned earlier. You can't discuss pantheism without mentioning my man, Baruch. He was huge. His masterpiece *Ethics*, published posthumously in 1677, is considered one of philosophy's all-time most influential works. A hundred years later, German philosopher Georg Wilhelm Friedrich Hegel (1770–1831) said, "You are either a Spinozist or not a philosopher at all." You know you're somebody when a new noun is formed using -*ist* at the end of your name.

The thing is, for a long while, everybody had to read *Ethics* in secret. Spinoza's discourse on pantheism was still highly controversial. In fact, it made it onto the *Index Librorum Prohibitorum*, the Catholic Church's list of forbidden books. Naturally, this made it like catnip to other thinkers of the day, but it wasn't even translated into English until the late 1800s (by novelist George Eliot, as a matter of fact).

So what did Spinoza have to say? Well, he started with a sort of ontological slant, declaring that God exists necessarily, and, further, being God, has an infinite number of attributes. We know only two: thought and extension, meaning, essentially, that the universe is an extension of God (but within God, who is all). In this way, one can conceive of God as having transcendent, universal, eternal qualities, and yet this is perfectly consistent with the changing natural world that we're able to access and live in. Spinoza rejected Descartes's mind–body dualism, believing that mind and body are one. And God, to Spinoza's way of thinking, is complete unto himself. There's not necessarily a purpose for the universe. It simply is. It has no need for anything more.

Now, Hegel wrote of *das Absolute*. The absolute. An all-inclusive, unifying whole. In fact, for Hegel, this unifying whole was a mind, and being that it is the absolute of everything, this means that everything is a mind or dependent on a mind—a philosophical position known as *absolute idealism*. Physical things are illusory. I admit to you that I have always found this position appealing. Why? Because if there's a God, why would he go to the trouble of "making" something like the universe? With a mind like God's, wouldn't you just sort of "think" the universe into existence? Doesn't it make more sense to imagine the universe within the mind of God than God having retreated to his workshop to cobble together a universe out of material he bought at some celestial

Home Depot? Hegel thought so. (You can see why Hegel was a fan of Spinoza.)

There has been a long and illustrious line of thinkers since then who have expressed a partiality to pantheism, including, interestingly enough, Henry David Thoreau and our man Walt Whitman. Thoreau felt he was born to be a pantheist, writing in his famous *Walden*, "Heaven is under our feet, as well as over our heads." And, of course, the snake handlers are all pantheists. Just kidding. I have *no* idea what they believe. But here's something that might surprise you: Albert Einstein was something of a pantheist and a big fan of Baruch. "We followers of Spinoza," he once wrote to a friend, "see our God in the wonderful order and lawfulness of all that exists." Now, I hedge, saying he was "something of" a pantheist. Truthfully, Einstein was known to say that the problem of God was "the most difficult in the world."

That's the thing about pantheism, or any theological worldview, it seems to me. How is it possible to get your mind around a concept as big as God? For pantheists, that's kind of the point. God is not only big; God is everything. And everything is God. I say we follow this intriguing philosophy a little further to see if it answers some of our questions and objections. If it does, great. If it doesn't, well, that's okay, too. You've got nothing better to do, right? Neither do I.

CHAPTER NINE

LIKE PANTHEISM, ONLY BETTER

I n the last chapter, we were introduced to a concept of God that might help explain some of the objections and paradoxes that are often raised regarding the more traditional Abrahamic concept of God. Pantheism, the belief that God is everything and everything is God, provides some interesting food for thought.

For one thing, if the universe is part of a timeless God, then we need not worry about the paradoxes of time. Pantheism also addresses the argument of divine hiddenness. Where's God? How about *everywhere,* that's where. Now, per John L. Schellenberg in Chapter 7, we might still wonder why a loving God wouldn't make sure those who are open to him come to believe, but we'll have to table that for now. We can at least say that God is no longer hidden. And the objection on the grounds of all the world's religions contradicting each other can now be more forcefully countered with the idea I had in the first place. They're all a part of God, and so they're all valid.

But wait, maybe that's a step too far. I suggested earlier that they might all be true to a certain extent. If everything is God, then they must be true completely. Are there any false ideas in pantheism? How can any idea—a part of the universe, a part of God, no less—be wrong? Well, Spinoza believed there *were* no wrong ideas; if an idea seems in contradiction to other ideas, it is merely being improperly related to them.

And that's fine as far as it goes, but if you really think it through (which an intelligent person like you is apt to do), that means we're saying that, in some context (limited though it might be), somewhere, sometime, somehow, even the Holocaust is a proper idea. Now, that doesn't mean it's good, but pantheism does mean that it's part of God. And that brings us to perhaps the biggest objection to pantheism. How to explain the problem of evil. If anything, we've now exacerbated it. If evil exists, and everything is contained within God, then God encompasses evil. Yikes. That doesn't seem right.

Philosophers have also pointed out that pantheism pretty much does away with any form of free will. We're not in any way separate from God. All our ideas are God's ideas. All our thoughts (even the evil ones) are God's thoughts. What is there of our individual selves?

Now, it must be said that neither of these objections—the presence of evil or the lack of free will—invalidates pantheism as a worldview. It might just be that evil is a part of God, and it might just be that we have no free will.

But if that's the universe, have we described a concept of God (or the universe, since they're the same in pantheism) that has any real appeal to it? Haven't we just substituted the word "God" with "universe"? Famed German philosopher Arthur Schopenhauer (1788–1860) thought so. "To call the world God is not to explain it," he said. "It is only to enrich our language with a superfluous synonym for the word 'world.'" Richard Dawkins put it more in the parlance of our time: "Pantheism is sexed-up Atheism."

But that's not entirely true. We're postulating something more than just the physical universe and calling it "God." We're postulating a universe of consciousness. An intelligent universe. This is what we're calling "God." Nevertheless, I do have to confess that I'm suddenly finding this worldview not very satisfying. If the universe is conscious and intelligent, and if we're going to call it "God," am I really going to regard with any kind of esteem a God that's apparently okay with the idea of the Holocaust? And damn it, I just don't feel like I'm devoid of free will.

On the other hand, I really like the way that pantheism allows for a participating God. Plus, it makes sense to me that our creation would be *a part* of God and not some separate project, like some intricate train set in some guy's basement. You know the guy. With his engineer hat? Pushing the transformer handle and watching the train snake around the little town he built until his wife calls him up for dinner? That guy? Probably named Jerry? That can't be God, right?

So is there a way to take this pantheism idea and somehow extend it into something that works better? Well, "extend" is an interesting word choice. There are those who believe that the universe is God but that God is also more than the universe. German philosopher Karl Christian Friedrich Krause (1781–1832) is generally credited with coining the word *panentheism*, meaning "all in God," although some scholars believe that the first usage can be credited to Friedrich Wilhelm Joseph Schelling (1775–1854), another German philosopher. Either way, panentheism is distinct from pantheism in that the former imagines a sort of dipolar God—a fixed, eternal, transcendent God; and an immanent, right-here, right-now God. As though God has extended himself, an extension that we experience as spacetime.

So how exactly would this work? Well, perhaps the best way for me to lay out an argument for panentheism is not to try to make one. I'm going to stay in my lane. What I'll do instead is recount the argument made by preeminent panentheist, and personal favorite philosopher of mine, Alfred North Whitehead (1861–1947). Whitehead was a mathematician by trade. With a former student of his, he wrote a tremendously important book, first published in 1910, entitled *Principia Mathematica*. Like most people, you no doubt keep a copy of this book on your nightstand. No, you don't. Nobody outside the field of mathematics would have any reason whatsoever to open this book. *Principia Mathematica* is an esoteric masterpiece of complexity dealing with symbolic logic and set theory. There are formulas in this book that use symbols I have never seen before. But for the committed math nerd, it's great stuff and a *very* influential work.

Here's something interesting about *Principia Mathematica*. Whitehead's cowriter? None other than Bertrand Russell, dedicated agnostic mentioned earlier. Theistically, however, Whitehead went in another direction. In the early 1920s, his interest drifted from math to metaphysics. In fact, he ultimately landed at Harvard as a professor of philosophy. And as influential as *Principia Mathematica* was in the field of mathematics, Whitehead's *Process and Reality*, published in 1929, is every bit as influential in the field of philosophy, if not more so.

It's also just as complex. How complex? I've read it, but I didn't read it unarmed. I used a study guide, and I make no apologies. In this, it is comparable in its near inscrutability to James Joyce's *Ulysses*, published seven years earlier. (Books were apparently way more complicated back in those days.) The difference is that *Process and Reality* actually makes sense and is intended to do so. (Here's what Joyce's wife Nora supposedly had to say to her husband about *Ulysses*: "James, why don't you write books people can read?" Mrs. Whitehead said no such thing to Alfred, as far as anyone knows.)

Anyway, allow me to at least take a stab at describing White-head's panentheistic worldview. Whitehead starts with the idea that there are two basic objects: those that are actual and those that are pure possibilities. The first he called *actual entities*, and the second he called *eternal objects*. Good for you to pick up on the idea that he relies on Plato here. Remember blue existing as a universal—a Platonic form? Well, that's what Whitehead is referring to when he talks about eternal objects. These are entities only in the abstract.

Now, actual entities start out as eternal, abstract objects. Nothing but potentialities. Blue is a universal until it is made manifest as a real color in the world. (Of course, there remains a perfect form of blue, which we can now perceive, filtered as that perception is by our minds.) But Whitehead wondered why some possibilities, some eternal objects, become actual, while others do not. There must be some metaphysical principle that determines what is made manifest. Or that, conversely, stops what can only be imagined to be an infinite number of potentialities from becoming actual. It would be a bit of a crowded universe if everything possible became real.[1] Whitehead calls this metaphysical principle *the principle of limitation*, or *determination*, or *concretion*. Ultimately, he uses another word to describe it: "God."

With God essentially deciding what is made manifest, we have a suggestion of value and purpose for the universe. But for White-head, there is also room for free will. Actual entities, or occasions, constitute the known universe. And from these entities, we get more and more sophisticated systems, such as, eventually, minds.

---

1. Interestingly, there's a philosophical point of view called modal realism, propounded by philosopher David Lewis (1941–2001), that believes just that: that all possible worlds are real.

Consciousness is an elaborate society or nexus, if you will, of actual entities. (Maybe the most elaborate.)

Each entity gathers information from past actual occasions *and* eternal objects—Whitehead calls this *prehending*, a sort of rudimentary form of apprehending—thus becoming something unique, something novel. This means a constantly changing universe, always in the process of becoming something new. This, in fact, is the "process" in *Process and Reality*. And for Whitehead, this creative process is everything. *Creativity* is the ultimate metaphysical principle in Whitehead's worldview. It underlies everything. Even God!

But wait—if all of this is within God, doesn't this mean a changing God? You betcha. God is part of the process, too. God is an actual entity, concretizing and/or limiting eternal objects. And if actual occasions prehend past occasions, then there is an interconnection between all occasions, including God. Everything in the universe is a consequence in some way of everything that has come before. And God is in the midst of it. So God is a changing God, not an eternal, unchanging God. Of course, this is a stunning claim that Whitehead makes. God *always* seems to be described as unchanging. Whitehead says nope.

Although God is in everything, and the divine pervades all things, that doesn't preclude the idea that, because of free will, there might also be something of the universe that is not, let us say, consistent with God's nature. (Or, using a New-Agey term that I happen to like, not "in alignment" with God's nature.) Remember, in panentheism, there is an eternal, unchanging God beyond the spacetime-extended God.

Humans might be of God, but we have some autonomy within God. Think of a school of fish. If you'd never been introduced to the concept of fish, and you happen suddenly to be underwater where you observe a school of hundreds of herrings, you might be tempted to think of that school as one single organism, so closely to each other do the herring swim, and in such consistent regimentation. They dart left and right in total solidarity. But each fish, if it really wanted to, could simply take off, zig while everybody else zags. They're all a part of the school, and there's something of the school within each one, but they're also independent.

But free will needn't mean being out of alignment with God. Free will can, and does, mean creativity, and creative acts may well be in alignment with God. Yes, everything is connected, but with the sophisticated complex of actual entities that make up a mind (human consciousness), there is always the potential for something new, something perhaps that God would never have planned. Think of God as the provider of the raw materials that the underlying creative process of the universe—a universe that is forever in the process of *becoming* rather than just *being*—uses to advance life forward into totally new ground. Human minds, although connected to the universe, operate uniquely and creatively, formulating new thoughts and ideas. New even to God! Humans become partners—with God—in creativity. God provides and observes.

And yet God remains the keeper of the eternal objects, too. This is the dipolar God that gives us a panentheistic system, a God with one foot in the eternal world and one foot in ours. Timeless, eternal truths and temporal, changing occasions. An eternal God, and an immanent God. A God suggesting purpose and value, and conscious minds free to move in other directions.

Got it? Okay, let's get away from Whitehead's terminology for a second and summarize this in more basic terms, just to bring it all home. God acts as the gatekeeper, allowing certain eternal forms into the universe (the color blue, for instance). God can do this because God is a real thing (or else how do eternal forms become actual?) *and* a part of the universe But also with access to the eternal stuff. Now, God has allowed in whatever concepts might be necessary to evolve matter into something as sophisticated as human consciousness. But as things evolve, things change. A human mind is the result, in at least some small way, of everything that has come before. And so there is a very real connection between all that is past and all that is present and all that is to come. It sounds deterministic, but the determinism stops at the present moment because the mind is influenced not just by past events but by all the eternal concepts (Plato's forms) that God has made available. Beauty, for instance. And so the mind becomes more than the culmination of past events. New ideas and thoughts are created. Maybe the mind, so influenced by beauty, decides to write a song or paint a seascape. Creativity results. The universe is altered. A song or a painting exists that didn't exist before.

The universe is trillions and trillions of these little occurrences every moment. It is constantly undergoing the creative process of change. Creativity runs the show. God sets it up; human consciousness plays it out. We are partners in God's creation.

God as a creative partner? This is not your grandfather's God.[2] And that is the point. Whitehead's god is not the bearded god in sandals sitting on a throne in the sky, apart from us, watching and judging. Whitehead's god is much more accessible to us than the bearded one. And much more affected.

Whitehead's process philosophy became process *theology* in the hands of a contemporary of his named Charles Hartshorne (1897–2000). Hartshorne was an American philosopher who taught at a variety of universities for a very long time, ultimately

---

2. Unless of course your grandfather is Alfred North Whitehead.

delivering his final lecture at the age of ninety-eight. He knew Whitehead personally, assisting him for a semester at Harvard in 1925. Hartshorne was heavily influenced by the older professor, although he disagreed on some of his finer points. He wasn't crazy about the term "eternal objects," for instance, preferring to think of potentialities as an indefinite continuum. In any case, Hartshorne became interested in the idea of a changing God from a theistic standpoint, keen on contrasting such a god with your standard view of God. It was Hartshorne, in fact, who used the very word "panentheism" to describe this view of reality with its dipolar deity, where Whitehead always described his philosophy using the word "process."

Another scholar influenced by Whitehead was theologian and philosopher John B. Cobb, Jr. (b. 1925). Cobb, author of fifty books, including *A Christian Natural Theology: Based on the Thought of Alfred North Whitehead*, would ultimately become the undisputed go-to Whitehead scholar. But Whitehead's influence has continued to grow among not just philosophers and theologians but even scientists and ecologists. And the reason is because of the possibilities that panentheism opens up with respect to ideas about the nature of God and the universe. And what are those possibilities? What would it mean exactly if God was not that immovable, inaccessible, unchanging bearded sky king most of us have been led to believe "He" is? Well. Let's you and I find out.

Chapter Ten

Not at All like Wayne

Panentheism postulates a god that is immanent yet eternal. We reside within this god. We are a part of this god. And this god is within us. But we have some degree of autonomy, and this autonomy is fundamental to the creative process that represents the continual progression of the universe.

All well and good. But let's not get too far ahead of ourselves. We've spent a fair amount of time discussing arguments for and against God's existence. Maybe we owe it to ourselves to see how this conception squares with these arguments. Does panentheism hold up? Or does it just sort of lie there, still and lifeless, like my cousin Wayne on the sofa in front of his TV, drinking beer, watching old *Bonanza* episodes on MeTV, and refusing to look for work, even though he is *three months behind* on his rent?

Let's begin with the pro arguments. You may have recognized a bit of the ontological argument in the process theology of panentheism. This is the argument that says that God must exist because the greatest of all beings *would* exist. First, we're starting with the Platonian idea that universals exist independent of human consciousness. This premise might be questionable in and of itself, but one can always appeal to the consciousness of God. Universals exist because God exists. But this is what philosophers call circular reasoning. Universals exist because God exists, and we know that

God exists because universals exist. This is not good philosophy. So to make it better, one could rely on the ontological argument and say that universals, or eternal objects, exist because we can see evidence of them in the actual world, and there's no way they could have been made manifest without something making them so, something actual. And that something must be God (Whitehead's principle of determination). God is, therefore, actual. No other thing, besides the greatest of all beings, could have this kind of power over universals.

Well, that's *kind of* the ontological argument. Sort of. But more than anything, it presents a method for how God created the universe, and that takes us back to the cosmological argument. I think process theology gives us a decent explanation for the beginning of things if we need one. God used the raw materials of eternal objects. But, you ask, where did the eternal objects come from? Well, as John Cobb, Jr. has pointed out, "For Whitehead 'eternal' means nothing more than nontemporal. That is another way of saying that 'eternal' objects have no actuality at all in themselves." In other words, nontemporal things are non-actual, and this means that it's up to God to bring them into existence in the universe. (One reason that Whitehead used the phrase *principle of concretization* to describe God.)

Now, we still don't avoid the problem of a timeless God performing a temporal act, even if that act is nothing more than "thinking" us into existence within his own mind. Then again, maybe time has always been a part of God. Thinking us into existence might have just created a new track of time. Yes, indeed, I rather like that idea. But either way, at least we've solved the problem of God participating within time and space: time and space are within God.

The argument from design holds up well, too, don't you think? Remember the chicken-and-egg quandary? How did life come about without the necessary information for life (DNA), and how did the necessary information come about without life? This information could well be part of God's raw materials, eternal ingredients that God made real. That explains that.

But what about the historical record argument? There are still all those contradictions. Well, sure, but if we agree that, with panentheism, there is some degree of individual free will, then perhaps that accounts for why we don't have a universally agreed-upon record. We're talking about humans writing scripture and sacred texts with minds that operate with some freedom. That's guaranteed to result in inconsistencies. But do inconsistencies mean that the records should all be ignored? Stay tuned. We'll address that in good time.

I liked the moral argument before, and I have to say I like it even more now. As mentioned, God deciding what is made manifest suggests value and purpose. Goodness, mercy, justice, compassion, benevolence, tolerance, reaching out and grabbing someone about to jump off a cliff in Hawaii, warning Chuck about the saber-toothed tiger behind him—these could all be sourced in God, eternal qualities introduced into the world. Not only that, but an all-in-God worldview means that everything and everyone is, in a very real way, connected. In that Joseph Campbell story of the cliff, the police officer almost sacrificed himself because—in the moment of his "one-pointed meditation"—he saw himself in the other. Of course he did. He *was* in the other, and the other was in him.

If morality is sourced in the actions of God deciding what is made manifest, so could beauty be likewise sourced. And love. And so the aesthetic argument is more compelling now, too. Pascal's wager and/or the existential argument? Well, maybe if one were beginning to lean toward the existence of God, these arguments might be more attractive, but that's not a decision I can make for you.

The prevalence of religious experiences is still very much on the table, but what about mind–body dualism? Well, here's where things get *really* interesting. Earlier, we argued that perhaps there is more to the universe than the physical world. Perhaps there is a world of consciousness. Panentheism (or pantheism, for that matter) creates the possibility of turning this thinking on its head. Instead of asking whether there's a world of consciousness, maybe we should be asking if there's really a physical world. And maybe the answer is no.

If the universe is within the mind of God, then there's no need for a physical world as we understand the idea. Physicality might only be a way in which the world is presented to us so that we can make sense of it. It might not be "real," or rather, it may only be "real" to our perceptions.

These thoughts would have been considered preposterous back in the simple days of classical atomic theory. The world was clearly physical, and this was easy to prove. If you broke everything down, it was all made up of physical particles called atoms. And, if you'll recall your high school chemistry class, each atom has a nucleus of neutrons and protons, orbited by electrons. And that's all there was.

Then came quantum theory. Now there are quarks and bosons and leptons and fermions and nerkles and bar-ba-loots.[1] Quantum physics is mind-blowing. In 1926, physicist Erwin Schrödinger,

---

1. Okay, so those last two are actually Dr. Seuss creations. But the rest are real, I swear.

quoted earlier, first suggested that elementary particles sometimes behave more like waves. This is the famous wave–particle duality. And it becomes really significant (and downright spooky) with what is called "the observer effect." Have you heard of this? There's something about actually observing one of these waves that collapses it into a particle. Makes it *physical*. Otherwise, quanta particles are basically waves of light. They're energy! So, if you take your chair and keep chopping it down into smaller and smaller pieces, you'll eventually break it into molecules, atomic particles, subatomic particles, and then... energy, with the presence of an observer (or some form of interaction with the external world) affecting the collective waves of energy, essentially turning the waves into a chair. Hey, I couldn't make this shit up. Google it if you don't believe me.

Now, I'm not about to use quantum physics to prove panentheism or to claim that the universe is conscious and not physical. No way. But I will say that the current state of the field of physics is at least not hostile to the idea. And the fact is, a universe within the mind of God explains the origin and presence of consciousness itself. Consciousness doesn't have to evolve from dead matter, because nothing of the universe is dead. Everything, being within the mind of God, is alive and conscious. Human minds are now explainable by Whitehead's idea of the evolution of more and more sophisticated systems, societies of actual—conscious—entities forming higher levels of consciousness culminating in human minds.[2]

In fact, there is no mind–body dualism. Like Spinoza, Whitehead believed Descartes was wrong. So mind–body dualism is

---

2. Or other minds. Who's to say there's not an alien race out there with a more elaborate nexus of consciousness? Probably there is, huh?

often used as a proof of God, but maybe it would be better to side with the atheists on the subject and claim that there is no dualism, no distinction between the mind and the brain. But not for the reason that atheists make the claim—not, that is to say, because there is no conscious mind or self. It's all brain matter, an atheist might say. But it might well be the opposite. There is no brain matter, just a conscious mind, because all matter is conscious. Physicality is only a useful perception.

This was Hegel's idealism, remember. George Berkeley thought similarly, believing that objects are mind-dependent. He, too, was what you might call an immaterialist. There's a closely related worldview called *panpsychism*, which is the belief that although objects might be physical, they are imbued with mentality, even consciousness.

Hey, I know these worldviews may seem out there, but the belief in a conscious universe is actually quite sane and comes with a longstanding, credible tradition. Panpsychism happens to be one of the oldest philosophical beliefs in the world, going back to Thales (c. 624–545 BCE), a Greek philosopher way before Plato. A conscious universe is inherent in Spinoza's pantheism. Our man William James (Mr. Pragmatic!) was a believer, writing, "Our physical perceptions are effects on us of 'psychical' realities." And it goes without saying that Whitehead felt the same way, as did Charles Hartshorne and John Cobb, Jr. And, of course, so do the snake handlers. (Again, kidding.)

The idea is even being talked about today in scientific circles. A recent gathering of physicists and philosophers took place at Marist College in Poughkeepsie, New York, to discuss the question of a conscious universe. Nothing was decided (typical in gatherings of scientists and philosophers), but the idea of even meeting about such a subject would have seemed absurd not that many years ago.

Anyway, I know that none of this—in and of itself—proves God, but the idea of a conscious universe fits nicely with panentheism, and that's the overall point.

Okay, so panentheism seems to confirm all of our earlier arguments for the existence of God. Or we can at least say it doesn't do anything to negate them or gunk them up too badly. But that's to be expected. The real test is how panentheism stacks up against the arguments *against* the existence of God. Well, let's see.

First, I think our new conception of God answers the argument of theological noncognitivism. Now that a definition of God has been produced, is it reasonable to claim that you don't know what I'm talking about? Now, you can still say that even with the concept presented here, there's still too much confusion, complexity, or mystery for anyone to seriously believe in this God we've described. And sure, I can understand that. God remains mysterious in countless ways. I mentioned before the difficulties of wrapping one's head around a concept as big as God. But there are a lot of things we don't understand and that remain mysteries to us. Like the Academy Award for Best Picture of 1999. Or consciousness. We've talked a lot about consciousness, and we know that all we have are theories. But we believe in consciousness, don't we? Even if we don't believe it exists, we still believe in its effects. We feel conscious. We experience things. We don't run around saying, "Sorry, I can't discuss consciousness because it's an unintelligible, unfathomable idea." So you can throw the theological noncognitivism card if you really want to, but I think that would be disingenuous of you.

Do you fare any better with the argument from divine hiddenness? Well, with panentheism, we now know where God is. God is everywhere. God is in everything. God is in you. God is in me.

Okay, you say, but if that's the case, can't he do something dramatic to confirm his existence? Per Schellenberg's concern, wouldn't he at least make himself apparent to those willing to believe? For that matter, why wouldn't he just write his name in the sky? Rent a series of billboards? Advertise during the Super Bowl? Morph into the shape of a human being and hold a press conference where he confirms that the panentheists are right?

A panentheist would answer in a way that may surprise you: no. No, God cannot do any of those things. Why the hell not? For the same reason that the God of the School of Herring couldn't possibly come down from "on high" and make an appearance in the midst of the school. The school *is* that god. And that god is the school. Now, the God of the School of Herring might also be more than that (transcendent), but he is nevertheless all wrapped up with the school *as one*.

If panentheism is correct, then God has created a universe within God's being that has been presented to us as a material world run by the laws of physics. Time has begun, and the rules have been set. God, in other words, has created a universe within himself, and that world is God, and God is that world. What sense can it make for God to make an appearance within God? It would be like you shrinking yourself down to make an appearance within your spleen. Try that, why don't you?[3] In the end, there are things that are logically impossible, and God, as per C. S. Lewis, cannot do the logically impossible.

---

3. Cinema buffs might remember the film *Fantastic Voyage* (1966), in which a crew of doctors on a submarine is shrunken down (along with the submarine) in order to enter a patient's bloodstream to save him from some physical ailment or disease or something. (Frankly, all I remember about the movie is the presence of Raquel Welch.) But even in the movie, nobody entered their *own* body.

This is a bit of a shocker, isn't it? Didn't see it coming, did you? God is invariably described as "all powerful." It's one of the first attributes people think of.

But perhaps it's not true.

Whoa, am I now arguing for deism? A belief in God as creator only? Now inaccessible?

No, no, and no. Remember what the universe is made of: God, or at least the consciousness of God. We are in the mind of God. God's consciousness is all throughout the universe, making the universe intelligent, and making that intelligence accessible through *our* consciousness. Remember those 165 million Americans, believing that they have in some way connected with something beyond their own minds? This seems a bit likelier if there's some sort of universal consciousness that is at the fundament of reality. God, you see, is right here all the time. God doesn't act. We act. It's that creative partnership idea. God sets the stage; human consciousness plays the part. And God watches. God experiences. God feels. Here, we can bring back the aesthetic argument to answer the problem of hiddenness. The beauty of a sunset. The power of a Beethoven symphony. "Where's God?" you ask. God might just be hiding in plain sight. I see God wherever I see beauty.

But hang on; we're getting ahead of ourselves. We were still in the middle of stacking up panentheism against the arguments against God's existence. The point is that there's no hiddenness problem anymore. (At least to those who are looking and open to what they see.) So what was next? Ah, yes, the argument that science explains everything. Well, I think we agree by now that that's not true, don't we? There are plenty of things that science explains, but there's a ton of things that it doesn't. We've also handled the contradictions-of-religion thing pretty well, I believe, with the idea that human consciousness has spent thousands of years trying to interpret, as best it can, the nature of the world in which we find ourselves. Each religion, in its own way, is and has been a *human* means by which to make sense of this thing called existence. Yes, there are some wild inconsistencies, but isn't it likely that these are the results not of God's presence but of our interpretation of that presence?

What of the argument of incompatible properties? Recall that these paradoxes came about from characterizations of God as unchanging, all-powerful, omniscient, and perfect. Let's take these one at a time. First, Whitehead's process philosophy is all about change. God is far from unchanging. Creativity, as we've said, is the ultimate metaphysical principle in Whitehead's worldview, underlying everything, including God. And creativity means change.

Second, we've just arrived at the conclusion that God is not all-powerful. God cannot hold a press conference. Nor is God omniscient, although this might not be entirely settled. With everything existing within the mind of God, God surely knows all that exists. But with constant change along the track of time and the free will of humans, God might not know the future. Who can say? There's a philosophical position called "open theism" in which it is maintained that God forgoes having knowledge of what humans will do in order to preserve free will. (Richard Swinburne is an open theist.) I think there's an argument to be made (and a damn fine one) that the mind of God would be able to calculate the infinite possibilities between today and tomorrow and arrive at what those possibilities will bring into existence before they do so. Alternatively, there's still the theory that time is an illusion, just a useful tool for us to make sense of the universe, in which case God knows the future because, from God's perspective, it's all right here right now. Either way, it doesn't really matter because even with that knowledge, God can't do much about it, because God, as we've concluded, is not all-powerful, the same way that the God of the School of Herring is not all-powerful.

What about God's perfection? A changing God, not all-powerful, and possibly not omniscient? This is perfection? Well, maybe. What does perfection mean? Your guess is as good as mine. It seems to me that it at least has to start with the idea of not being negated by paradoxes, so maybe we're on the right track. Anyway, this is a question we can address in time. I'm not seeing it as a roadblock to God's existence so much as a question about God's nature.

Okay, so is that everything? Have we addressed all the arguments against God's existence? Well, not quite. The careful reader[4] will note that the biggest objection—the problem of evil—has been mostly glossed over. We've said some things about free will and God not being able to interfere, but this needs to be elaborated on, doesn't it? If I were you, I'd demand it. This is a huge deal, after all. For even if you're warming up, however slowly, to the idea that there might be some sort of intelligence behind the universe, what kind of intelligence would create a world in which bad things happen? Why should we even care about this intelligence? Well, meet me in the next chapter and we'll dive into this whole "evil" subject a little deeper.

---

4. That's you.

Chapter Eleven

The Deal on Evil

T he theory of God so far put forth in this book answers a lot of questions, but the problem of evil is still something of a conundrum. Even if the presence of evil is explained by God's inability to interfere in human affairs, there's still the question of why God would create a world where evil is allowed in the first place.

One way to answer is to invoke a variation on the simple philosophical argument from earlier: evil exists because good exists, as dark exists because light exists. The counterpart idea. But the variation is that the counterpart doesn't *have* to exist. Rather, the counterpart of good (evil) was made manifest not by God but by humankind. Once God permitted, let's say, kindness into the universe, this opened the door for unkindness—meanness, even cruelty. This doesn't mean that God gave cruelty a free pass at the door. It means that humans became able to act in kindness but, because of free will, were also able to act in the opposite way.

Give yourself two bonus points if you recognize anything of the Eden narrative here. The theme of the story, and of similar myths (such as what is found in *The Epic of Gilgamesh*), is that God provided a paradise that humankind turned away from through disobedience. Hence, we, as represented as Adam and Eve in the Old Testament, were cast out of that paradise. To relate it to our discussion here, God provided a wealth of beautiful concepts. But the moment we turned them on their heads and acted oppositely, paradise was over. This was the original sin, you see. Our creative partnership isn't always so good. God provides, we do our thing, and new concepts are created, including bad ones. But that's the price of both creativity and free will.

Now, free will isn't necessarily a given. We've been talking about it, and maybe the time has come to discuss it a bit more. Some people don't even believe in it. Hard, or causal, determinists believe that your next action, even your next thought, is a result of everything that has come before. Because of this, your actions aren't free. Each moment is predicated entirely on all the moments that have led to it, and you really have no choice as to what you're going to do or think next.

Naturally, Spinoza was a determinist, not necessarily because of the logic of every moment leading inexorably to the unalterable next but because as a pantheist believing that all is God, he couldn't imagine we'd have any choice in our actions. Everything, including our thoughts, is *of* God. Panentheists, on the other hand, have no such qualms. We can do things that are not of God's eternal nature. We can zig when everybody else zags.

But how to escape the logic of the hard determinists? Well, some thinkers, Descartes among them, believed in what's become known as "metaphysical libertarianism." Keep in mind that Descartes believed that there was more to the universe than the physical world. With consciousness, we are not beholden to physical causality. Our minds are free. The brain, composed of physical matter, might inevitably be directed to its next iteration, but the mind can override this seeming inevitability. And if we believe that everything is conscious, this becomes even more possible.

There's no escaping, however, the idea that we are governed, to a large degree, by circumstances and external constraints. Schopenhauer put it like this: "Man can do what he wills but he cannot will what he wills." What did he mean? He meant that we can act according to a motive or desire, but we're not free to choose the motive or desire. The nature of our motives is determined.

I can get on board with this. We are, it seems to me, products of our personalities, which have been laboriously shaped by our genes, upbringing, parents, friends, society, childhood experiences, etc. By the time we've reached *this* particular point, we're pretty much locked in, for good or for bad, on what we're going to strive for in life and who we're going to be and how we're generally going to behave. We can adjust the details, which is to say the tiny actions we take, but we're really beholden to a large degree to our personalities.

Long, long ago, when I was in sales, I used to attend motivational seminars. Motivational types make a big deal about how you can be whoever you want to be. It's all within! If you're not happy with your life, you can change! You can change yourself! Starting this minute! Today is the first day of the rest of your life! And other insipid platitudes!

These seminars would get me all pumped up. I'd walk away feeling energized and ready to become the great person I knew I could become. I would change all my bad habits. I would become a new man! Look out, world!

This feeling would sometimes last as long as two days. And then it would wear off, and I would find myself still pretty much the same person I was before the seminar. Only poorer by the amount I'd spent on it. And the accompanying tapes. And the workbook.

But I digress. The fact is, the best we might be able to do is to learn who we are, accept ourselves for that, be aware of our strengths so that we can emphasize them, and be even more aware of our foibles and weaknesses so that we can find whatever workarounds are available to minimize their damage. We're stuck with who we are, but at least we have *some* freedom in our actions because of our conscious minds, which are free. Consciousness means (some) free will.

Which means, of course, that we're free to choose cruelty over mercy. But two questions readily present themselves. First, who gets to define these terms? One person's cruelty might be another person's mercy. Or, more appropriate to our discussion, one person's good might be another person's evil. Is there, with the God of panentheism, an objective ethic? Well, if we accept Whitehead's theory that God acts as principle of limitation, allowing in only what's good, then the answer to that question would seem to be yes, there's an objective ethic. Good is what God has made manifest. Evil is what we have made manifest by acting in contradiction to it. Could you argue that God is an accessory for allowing us to act in contradiction to what is good? Well, maybe. But then you'd have to argue that you're an accessory for handing over your car keys to a guy pretending to be a parking attendant who then goes on to steal your car.

Importantly, good and evil, objective though they might be, are often far from obvious to us. The civil courts are full of parties suing each other because their respective definitions of "good" were somehow opposed to each other. Maybe the motivations of both parties in any given case really are good. Seven billion people jostling about on this globe pretty much guarantee conflict, and most of the time, it starts with good intentions, or at least it doesn't start out with bad ones. What happens when it's *Good v. Good*? Good can seem pretty damn subjective. And illusive.

The second question is even more fundamental. Who says the universe's baseline is good? We've said that evil exists because good exists. But can't you claim the opposite is the case? Maybe a being like Satan created the universe. There's a thought experiment among philosophers called "the evil God challenge," which asks why a good God should be likelier than an evil God. Maybe God brought into existence all the evil concepts available. Humankind decided to be nice one day and, bam, goodness arrived, but no thanks to the creator.

Maybe to answer these questions, we should remember Whitehead's assertion that the ultimate metaphysical principle underlying all, including even God, is Creativity (which, you'll notice, I've even decided to recognize by capitalizing). And clearly, that's in evidence in a process universe. The universe began as a creative act, and now we are continuing the creative process, continually bringing new things into reality that did not exist before. No matter what your theological beliefs are, it's hard to deny that Creativity drives pretty much everything.

In this light, perhaps it's more relevant to speak not in terms of "good" or "evil" but of "creative" or "destructive." Maybe these are the standards. "Good" can be defined as that which is creative, and "evil" can be defined as that which is destructive. Murder is destructive. Arson is destructive. War is destructive. Rape, robbery, assault, psychological abuse—all destructive. All evil.

Then again, there is a such thing as creative destruction. Tearing down an abandoned, dilapidated, and even hazardous house so as to build a new one. Not evil. Even killing might be considered creative if, for instance, it's done in self-defense to preserve a life or a country, the preservation of which will engender further creativity. Sometimes, something that appears destructive at first glance might go on to give birth to something exceedingly creative. This is the nature of a constantly changing universe.

It may be, in fact, that there are no general absolutes. It's hard to imagine the Holocaust being classified as anything other than destructive, but other historical moments might not be so clear. The American Civil War resulted in over 600,000 deaths and was exceedingly destructive, but it brought to a close, in the only real way possible at the time, the terribly destructive practice of slavery.

It might be that "good"/"evil" and "creative"/"destructive" are terms that can be recognized only given the complete context of a situation. Assuming, as proposed in the last chapter, that God is able to consider the zillions of events in any given day and accurately project the infinite possibilities that each event gives rise to (and there's no reason to believe, if you've come this far, that God would not be able to do this), it would naturally follow that God would know, in any given situation, what the ultimate, most creative, best long-term choice would be. That is to say, God would know which is the "good" choice. If so, then although there might not be general absolutes, there would be specific absolutes for each and every occasion.

For the individual, determining what the most creative, right, good thing to do in any personal situation would mean, essentially, being in alignment with God. How does one do this? Well, spiritual types will tell you that this is where prayer and meditation come in. Or perhaps direction and even examples from those religious texts we talked about. Or maybe just listening to your gut. With panentheism, God is within, remember. A spiritual person might suggest that we can know the mind of God on any given question because we can connect with God through our conscious selves. This isn't God speaking, mind you, or otherwise participating. It's someone simply tapping into the wisdom that's already there. The wisdom that's always been there.

Conversely, it's just as possible to ignore the wisdom within and take an action that is decidedly not in alignment with God. And there's your explanation for evil.

Interestingly, and significantly, if this worldview is accurate, it means that God *does* participate, albeit indirectly. God's wisdom is projected through us. What we do affects God, and God's wisdom passes back through us in what Whitehead called a "reciprocal relation." God participates through you and me. Alfred North Whitehead could be complicated, but he could also be eloquent: God "does not create the world, he saves it. Or, more accurately, he is the poet of the world, with tender patience leading it by his vision of truth, beauty, and goodness."

Put that in your pipe and smoke it.

Well, of course, this is all well and good for an explanation of how humans bring about evil. But what of the other tragedies? The tornadoes and hurricanes and floods and mud slides and earthquakes and tsunamis and fires? "Natural evils," as the philosophers put it, as opposed to "moral evils." As I write this, the death toll for a recent earthquake in Turkey and Syria, an event that took mere seconds to play out, has surpassed 50,000, a number that is almost impossible to get one's head around.

Assuming a God impelled by Creativity, the question answers itself. It must be because there was *no other way* to construct a *creative* universe. God, as keeper of the raw materials, brings into existence that which is capable of evolving into that which will give rise to human consciousness and a world that will make sense to us, a world that will be governed by logical, physical laws. A world where two plus two will always equal four. Among other things, this means a universe in which planets will form with geological attributes that will be conducive to life. With atmospheres likewise. Rain is a necessity, but aside from producing crops, rain can produce floods. Wind circulates warm and cool air, distributes seeds, and disperses pollutants. But wind can also come in the form of hurricanes and tornadoes. Our world isn't a creative world without the disruptive acts of nature.

Or the fragility of the human body. Heart disease, cancer, Alzheimer's, diabetes, malaria, typhus, COVID-19—how, you ask, is all of this explainable? As of this writing, COVID-19 has killed 7 *million people worldwide.* More than were killed in the Holocaust. Why would the universe be built in such a way as to allow such destruction? Well, if Creativity is a cycle of death and rebirth, then the old must make way for the new. The human body, like every other living organism on the planet, must begin to deteriorate, or else all 117 billion people who have ever been born would still be hanging around. Do you have any idea how far in advance you'd have to make dinner reservations at a nice restaurant if 117 billion people lived here? The human body is, of necessity, vulnerable. From the moment a person is born, that person's body is programmed to eventually self-destruct. That some bodies do this sooner rather than later most certainly seems unfair. There is no escaping this sentiment by even the coldest of hearts. But this is the price paid for a universe that is always in the process of change, that is always under the governorship of Creativity. And remember that nothing is ever lost. Not really. It's a world of interconnected consciousness, after all. Consciousness that simply re-forms itself. Nature is self-sustaining, we are a part of nature, and nature is a part of God.

Could it have been another type of world? Well, maybe, but it's hard to imagine, isn't it? For all we know, maybe there *is* another world somewhere where the sun always shines, the sky is always clear (except at night when just the right amount of rain falls while everyone is asleep), the wind is always gentle, the temperature is always 72 degrees, the ground never moves, and the same people live there forever, enjoying perfect health but never reproducing, thus giving everyone plenty of space and a guaranteed seat at their preferred eatery at any time. But that's not our world.

All of this, however, brings up a more fundamental question that you might now have on your mind. If we're contemplating a god that is, as mentioned above, able to accurately project the infinite possibilities that any event might give rise to, then surely this god had to know that the universe would go the way it did. Earthquakes would kill people. Armies led by evil fascists would kill many more people. Disease would ravage the population. So why? Why this world, with these possibilities? Why create a world *at all* if you can't create a peaceful, happy world? Why go through with it? Just for the sake of creativity?

Good question. A peaceful, happy world would always be preferable. I mean, that's a no-brainer. If you can't have that, why bother? It's why I always seek out peaceful, happy films whenever I go to the movies. I want to munch on my popcorn and watch smiling people talking nicely to each other, with very little happening in the way of plot. Perhaps the beautiful main characters are strolling through a colorful garden in the sunshine. But not too much sunshine. I don't want to see anybody getting sunburned. Yep, that's my kind of movie.

No, wait—that's not my kind of movie at all. And it's probably not yours. Set aside Creativity for the moment. We want to *experience* life, don't we? Really experience it. And remember, through us, God experiences, too. God feels. And this not only explains the why of *this* world, but the why of creating any world. To experience. To feel. We're front and center to the greatest drama ever produced. A drama full of highs and lows, joys and sorrows, humor and pathos, cruelties and mercies, failures and victories, war and peace, anger and compassion.

Love and hate.

Life and death.

And we do not only get to play the characters in this drama; we get to have some say over how to play the parts.

But we're not on stage all alone. God feels everything we feel. God feels the joys; God feels the pains. "God," Whitehead wrote, "is the great companion—the fellow sufferer who understands."

In this light, evil is redeemed.

Of course, you don't have to be a believer in God to appreciate life's ups and downs and to recognize the beauty of a world that has both joy and sorrow. One of the great thinkers of the twentieth century, French philosopher, Nobel Prize winner, and atheist Albert Camus (1913–1960), believed that life was worth embracing in all of the absurd ways it is presented to us, and I don't use the word "absurd" frivolously. That was the very word he used. Camus was a committed absurdist. Life made no sense to him. That is to say, there was no external justification for it. But that didn't mean you couldn't find meaning.

In his classic *The Myth of Sisyphus*, Camus starts by declaring that there is only one truly serious philosophical problem: suicide. In an absurd life, do we end it all, or do we live it anyway? In the end, he advocates for "revolt," rebelling against life's absurdity and living it to its fullest. His "revolt" idea is actually an acceptance. An acceptance of the absurd. Screw it, he says. He invokes Sisyphus, the character in Greek mythology who was forever condemned to roll a boulder up a hill, only to see it roll back down where he would have to start rolling it back up again. A meaningless, absurd condition of life, if ever there was one. But, you know, even for the brief moment that Sisyphus makes it to the top, the view must be grand, huh? Maybe it's worth the effort. Camus went further. He thought that the *effort* was worth the effort. "The struggle itself toward the height is enough to fill a man's heart," Camus wrote. And then he concluded, "One must imagine Sisyphus happy."

The existence of God suggests the external meaning that Camus found missing, but that doesn't mean he was wrong about the absurdity of life. Damn it, it *is* absurd. I think anybody giving the matter just a little reflection will find it hard to escape this conclusion. What kind of a world are we living in where millions of people can be exterminated by genocide, tens of thousands can be killed in an instant by the shifting of the ground, and multitudes can be decimated by a pandemic? Well, we're living in the only world available to us—*that's* what world. A world where we're each rolling our own individual boulders up that hill.

But absurd doesn't have to mean bad. We're *in the play*. We're performing our parts to the best of our abilities. And God is alongside, seeing everything we see and feeling everything we feel, feeling the absurdity but living our lives with us for the sake of, well, living our lives with us. And accepting the bad with the good, for they are inextricably linked.

C. S. Lewis lost his wife to bone cancer and went into deep grief. But in his grief, his faith was ultimately strengthened when he thought back not to his wife's death but to their lives together, at which point he felt gratitude for having experienced true love. He talks about it in his book *A Grief Observed*, and his sentiments are dramatized beautifully in the film *Shadowlands* where his part is played masterfully by Anthony Hopkins. "The pain now," Hopkins's Lewis says, in contemplating the death of his wife, "is part of the happiness then. That's the deal."

Chapter Twelve

Eastern Religions for $200, Alex

S o how do you feel? Has the needle moved at all? If you think
back to where your mind was when you started reading this
book, are you any closer to opening your mind to the idea that God
exists and is good?

There's no need to answer just yet. After all, all this talk of a
panentheistic god, a god both transcendent and immanent, a god
who laughs and mourns with us, a god that is, perhaps, within us,
as we are within this god—if this is all true, if this strange worldview is somehow accurate, if this concept of *God* is even remotely
representative of reality, then this brings up a pretty significant
question; namely, why don't the major religions of the world—the
institutions whose very job it is to interpret God—why don't *they*
believe this?

How could all these religions have missed the big story?

Well, are we sure they did? Maybe if we examined them a little,
we might find some common ground between their theologies
and our panentheistic, process worldview. Hinduism provides an
interesting example. This religion has four sacred canonical texts,
known as the Vedas. One of these, the Rig Veda, includes a hymn
called the *Purusha Sukta*, which deals with the "Purusha," a complicated word without a direct equivalent in English, but which
can mean "cosmic consciousness" or "universal principle." Either

way, the Purusha is a divine entity, and the hymn, written thousands of years ago but still popular in Hinduism, proclaims that "all creatures constitute but one-quarter of him. Three-quarters of him are the immortal in heaven." And thus, the description of this divine Purusha invokes transcendence and immanence both.

In fact, according to Loriliai Biernacki, professor of religious studies at the University of Colorado and co-editor of *Panentheism across the World's Traditions*,[1] Hinduism (the oldest living religion on Earth, dating to 2000 BCE or earlier), with its multiplicities, offers one of the easiest, most fluent representations of a panentheistic worldview anywhere. As it turns out, Hindu tantric traditions (even tantric sex!) are all about bringing the divine into the world, bringing the transcendent into the here and now, and, by so doing, lifting oneself into the transcendent. One's self remains here, but one also moves beyond the self.

Tantric philosopher Abhinavagupta (c. 950–1016) was a mystic and theologian from Kashmir who wrote about the relationship of the world with the divine. His *Discourse on Suddenly Recognizing God* puts forth a seamless unification of the transcendent and the immanent. Abhinavagupta regarded Shiva, the supreme being in his Hindu theology (there are others in other theologies, such as Vishnu in the Vaishnavism tradition), as containing *within himself* all the world. Sound familiar? "I bow to him who pierces through and pervades with his own essence this whole, from top to bottom, and makes this whole world to consist of Shiva, himself."

Now, Abhinavagupta differed from another Indian scholar who came before him by a couple hundred years, Adi Shankara (c.

---

1. Oxford University Press, 2013, co-edited by Philip Clayton, an absolutely wonderful work that I have leaned on heavily in this chapter and in chapter 14.

700–750). Shankara believed in two separate worlds: the world of Brahman, which is the unchanging reality that is the divine ground of everything, and Maya, which is the world that we experience. Maya is an illusion. Brahman is the real world. Maya, therefore, needs to be rejected. Abhinavagupta saw it differently. The world we experience is real but part of a larger reality. Enlightenment, as Biernacki puts it, means recognizing our oneness to the whole world, not just that which appears to us. In this way, we participate in God's transcendence.

Meanwhile, the Bhagavad Gita, a 700-verse piece of the Sanskrit epic the *Mahābhārata*, talks of the world—all the gods within (Hindus have some 330 million, and no, that is not a misprint) as well as living beings—as being part of the divine body but insists that the divine being contains more than the world.

Clearly, in other words, there is a panentheistic point of view to Hinduism, a point of view that was alluded to in its sacred texts thousands of years before the word "panentheism" even originated in the West.

A much smaller Indian religion, Jainism (5 million adherents to Hinduism's 1.2 billion, with its roots dating back to around 500 BCE), is illustrative because of its direct parallel with Whitehead's process philosophy. Jainism emphasizes the idea that there is life (one might say consciousness) in everything. According to the *Ācārāṅga Sūtra*, an ancient Jain text, "There are living beings living in the earth, living in grass, living on leaves, living in wood, living in cow dung, living in dust-heaps." Yes, even in cow dung and dust-heaps! According to Christopher Key Chapple (Loyola Marymount University),[2] "This definition of soul or living being

---

2. Doshi Professor of Indic and Comparative Theology.

announces an omnipresence of life and soul.... In this sense, Jainism is truly panentheistic, seeing the presence of soul in all things."

Chapple notes the direct similarity with Whitehead's idea of prehension in the Jain idea of karma, which is not unlike the Hindu or Buddhist concept of karma. Each soul is on a journey through successive lives. And it takes what is learned from past lives, and the attendant karma thereof, to become its next iteration, much like an actual occasion prehending past events to become something new. "Each individual actual entity," wrote Whitehead, "contributes to the datum from which its successors arise." For the Jain religion, writes Chapple, "Each human action (karma) leaves a residue that carries over into future experience." Aren't these thoughts the same?

Sikhism, with close to 30 million followers, is another Indian religion with panentheistic leanings. Sikh scriptures have been interpreted as teaching nonduality—no separation between the God that Sikhs believe in (and they believe in only one) and the everyday world.

In China, we have Confucianism, based, of course, on the teachings of the great Chinese philosopher Confucius, who lived from 551 to 479 BCE but taught cultural lessons he derived from dynasties that preceded him by 1500 years or so. Traditional Confucianism didn't concern itself very much, if at all, with anything we would recognize as the divine, but Chinese philosophers Han Yu (768–824 CE) and Li Ao (772–841 CE) developed a more metaphysical system of Confucianism that became known as Neo-Confucianism. Then, philosopher and poet Zhu Xi came along (1130–1200 CE) to develop the Cheng-Zhu school of Neo-Confucius thought, and here's where things get more interesting.

Zhu Xi believed in a non-dualist metaphysics that encompasses "psychophysical energy" and something called "pattern." Hyo-Dong Lee (Drew University)[3] notes that psychophysical energy, a concept found throughout Eastern religion, is the primordial energy of the universe, constituting whatever exists. "[It's] what underlies and constitutes the dynamic creative process of the universe, encompassing both one and many, object and event, organic and inorganic, ideal and material, mind and body, spirit and nature." Pattern is the metaphysical ultimate "on which the creativity of [psychophysical energy] is dependent." Pattern is a continual activity of arranging and organizing, and it can't be separated from that which it acts upon. Pattern is also referred to as "the Great Ultimate." It is "the ultimate structure or 'logic' of everything that is and consequently affirms the Great Ultimate's universal presence in every single [thing]." Neo-Confucian Korean philosopher Nongmun Im Seong-Ju (1711–1788) further expanded on this, declaring that both psychophysical energy and the Great Ultimate are actual.

Importantly, Neo-Confucians make a distinction between what they call "the human heart-mind" and "the heart-mind of the Way," with the heart-mind of the Way describing the proper, harmonious road of the heart-mind. Sort of like being in alignment. But the human heart-mind has agency (free will). Can you see the process universe? The parallels between God and the Great Ultimate, consciousness and psychophysical energy, each acting upon the other, engaged in a never-ending process of creativity?

We've already mentioned Buddhism in the context of discussing the no-self, a concept that echoes within their concept of time. The present moment is holy ground for a Buddhist, and it is imperma-

---

3. Associate Professor of Comparative Theology.

nent. All is impermanence for a Buddhist. The First Noble Truth of Buddhism is that life is suffering. The Second Noble Truth is that life is suffering because we do not understand impermanence. We keep thinking that the good stuff (or bad stuff, for that matter) is going to last forever. You want to talk about process? The Buddhist worldview is nothing but process.

Is it also a panentheistic religion? Well, Geoffrey Samuel (Cardiff University)[4] makes the argument that, yes, it is. He makes a case similar to Loriliai Biernacki's case for Hinduism, i.e., the tantric practices of bringing the transcendent into the here and now. As Samuel puts it, "The world is repeatedly transformed from its ordinary, unenlightened (though by no means purely material) form into something pervaded by a divine essence, with which the practitioners themselves are directly related." Transcendent and immanent. Now, Buddhists don't believe in God per se, at least as most Westerners think of God. Instead, God is the highest truth and reality, through which the universe exists. Kind of like, well, God in a Whiteheadian universe, Shiva in Hindu theology, or the Great Ultimate in Confucianism. Are these different words for the same thing?

We could say a word here about Taoism, too. *Tao* is Chinese and means "way" or "path." Taoism's most famous text is the *Tao Te Ching*, thought to have been written by an ancient Chinese philosopher named Lao Tzu, who was believed to have lived somewhere around 600 BCE. The Tao (or Dao, as it's sometimes spelled) is essentially the ground of everything, the ultimate principle that defines reality. Now, Taoism is regarded as pantheistic, not panentheistic. Nevertheless, it exemplifies a completely different worldview from what we see in the West.

---

4. Emeritus Professor of Religious Studies.

So why, you ask, are we spending time on Eastern religions? (I'll bet you're a Westerner if you're asking this.) Because Eastern religions are obviously unique in their conceptions of God. Can you see through this discussion how that is? Contrast these conceptions of ultimate reality with the Western, patriarchal, anthropomorphic view of God, He of the beard and sandals, the ultimate king sitting on his golden throne in the sky, watching us dispassionately, judging us, making a Santa-Claus-like list of those who are good and those who are bad, allowing some of his subjects into Heaven and casting the rest of his subjects into Hell forever. What kind of God is that? Seriously. It would be bad enough if such a god were only nonsensical in a philosophical or epistemological way. But this god doesn't even make sense theologically. (Whitehead said this idea of ascribing kingly traits to God was "rendering unto God that which belongs to Caesar." Ha!)

So am I saying we should dismiss the patriarchal religions, the so-called religions of the Book, the Abrahamic religions, the Big Three: Islam, Judaism, and Christianity? Has this book been surreptitiously leading you to mysterious Eastern theologies? Well, not so fast. As it happens, we might just find that the Abrahamic religions have far more in common with our panentheistic, process universe concept than you can imagine. But first, we need to address another way in which these religions are often considered: the stubborn yet dangerously wrongheaded belief that each is, respectively, according to its most pious adherents, the truth, the whole truth, and nothing but the truth.

CHAPTER THIRTEEN

TAKING THE "FUN" OUT OF FUNDAMENTALISM

W hen it comes to the three big patriarchal religions, one character plays a critical role: Abraham. He's the founding father of Judaism, the first real spiritual role model for Christians, and an important prophet for Muslims. He's the common denominator at the beginning of the grand historical traditions of each of these three faiths. They went in different directions after Abraham, but their scriptures all recognize this key figure and hence they are often referred to as "the Abrahamic religions" or (by Muslims mostly) as the religions "of the Book," meaning of the scripture.

With 1.9 billion adherents and growing, Islam is the second biggest religion in the world. Christianity is the first, but a recent Pew Research publication predicts that the two will be neck and neck by the year 2050. So, what do Muslims (adherents of Islam) believe? Well, basically, they believe that Judaism and Christianity made fine religions at one time, but their major contributions were to lead the world to Islam. Both religions provided decent prophets, like Abraham, Moses, and (in the case of Christianity) Jesus, but then Muhammad came along as the last prophet, the one with the final say. Muhammad was born somewhere around 570 CE. God (Allah) revealed Himself to Muhammad over a period of years, starting when Muhammad was around forty, in divine messages that were written verbatim and organized into 114 chapters known as the Quran. For a devout Muslim, the Quran is *it*. Well, along with the Hadith, a collection of sayings and deeds of Muhammad. All the world's religious or divine truths are in these holy texts, even the laws that humankind should live under.

For the *really* devout Muslim, this makes all other religions wrong. Moreover, all adherents of the other religions should stop believing in their religions and start believing in Islam. In fact, for radical believers, all the world should come under Allah's sovereignty. For them, life is an ongoing battle between the good of Islam and the evil of secular and other theological societies. There is no middle ground. Moreover, in a Final Judgment, the faithful Muslims will be the only ones admitted to Heaven; all others will be consigned to Hell.

We might call these believers "fundamentalists." But fundamentalism is not unique to Islam, as you no doubt already know. If you reread the last paragraph and substitute the word "Christian" for "Muslim," "Christianity" for "Islam," and "Christ" for "Allah," you'll end up with a definition of Christian fundamentalism. There is Jewish fundamentalism, too. Orthodox Judaism insists on strict adherence to Jewish law. There are even so-called ultra-Orthodox Jews. Haredi Judaism is the most conservative branch, eschewing much of the modern world. Like Islamic and Christian fundamentalists, Orthodox Jews can be militant and political. Religious Zionists are Orthodox Jews throughout the world who advocate for the security of Israel, believing it to be land promised by God just to them.

Now, a word has to be said here about my use of the term *fundamentalism*. It's a broad term that can nevertheless have specific meanings, depending on who's using it. For our purposes, I would submit that fundamentalism can be identified first and foremost by its exclusionary nature. A fundamentalist is a believer in a worldview that excludes all other worldviews from the possibility of being true. Consequently, a fundamentalist believes that the people of his or her faith have a monopoly on God; God's attention and love are drawn more or less exclusively to them. They are God's people. Moreover, they are the ones to whom God will grant salvation and a Heavenly afterlife.

One common hallmark of fundamentalism is *literalism*. Whether it's Islam, Christianity, or Judaism, literalists argue that taking scripture—divinely inspired as it is—any way other than literally opens the door for human interpretation and human interpretation leads to improper readings of the scriptures. They argue this without realizing, apparently, that choosing to take any given scripture literally is itself a form of interpretation. We all interpret. That's how we experience life. Which is why, even among literalists, you can find disagreements over scripture.

Moreover, literalists tend to ignore the fact that ancient narratives, going back to Homer and before, were very often written using great symbolism, metaphor, and allegory. It was the literary style of the time. Consequently, it's a good bet that the ancient scriptures of the holy texts of the Abrahamic religions were written, at least to some degree, this way, too. Perhaps, to pick an example, a man named Jonah didn't *really* spend three days and three nights in the "belly of a great fish." Perhaps the story was meant as a metaphor, just as tales in the *Odyssey* were meant to impart wisdom using the form of compelling stories. Maybe Jesus didn't really feed thousands of people with just a few loaves of bread. Maybe that story was meant metaphorically, too. (Perhaps it represents the idea of people being fulfilled by the words or teachings of Jesus.)

What literalists fail to realize is that metaphor and symbolism can be more powerful than literalism. Much more powerful. That's why great writers throughout history have made use of these tools. It's why Shakespeare wrote, "But, soft! What light through yonder window breaks? / It is the east, and Juliet is the sun." Or why Tom Cochrane wrote, "Life is a highway / I wanna ride it all night long."[1] Juliet isn't really the sun, and life isn't really a highway, but the metaphors carry power. It's a way to show instead of just tell. Every beginning writing course preaches showing, not telling, because showing engages the reader so much more emotionally.[2] Why *wouldn't* the writers of the holy texts make use of such tools? Moreover, do you know any real-life people who speak *exclusively* in literal terms? There's a reason we find the Amelia Bedilia children's books funny: Amelia takes everything literally. If you want to tell her to dust the furniture, you'd better tell her what you really mean—you want her to *un-dust* the furniture. Otherwise, you're likely to get a completely different result.

The exclusivity factor in fundamentalism provides its own problems. It's not hard to see the damage it's done throughout history. If you Google "religious wars" or "holy wars," you'll find lists of wars throughout the history of humankind that have killed millions of people, with each side of each war convinced that God was right behind them all the way (and necessarily against their enemies). The Crusades, a series of wars launched primarily by Christians to gain control of holy lands in the Middle East and lasting from around 1095 to 1291, were responsible for an estimated

---

1. I wonder if anyone's ever put William Shakespeare and Tom Cochrane together before. Am I the first?

2. "Don't tell me the moon is shining," wrote famed Russian playwright Anton Chekhov, "show me the glint of light on broken glass."

1.7 million deaths. The Christian Inquisition, running from the mid-thirteenth century to the nineteenth century and established to root out heretics (people who, for whatever reason, simply did not believe in the prevailing religious wisdom of the times), was responsible for the executions of thousands, often after they were tortured. Christian fundamentalism has toned down, but it hasn't gone away. And, like the fundamentalists of the past, today's fundamentalists are very keen on taking political stances and driving governmental policies based on their exclusionary beliefs.

Islamic fundamentalism has led to Sharia law—based on literal *interpretations* of scripture—which you can find here in the twenty-first century in many countries throughout the Middle East. Sharia law includes the veiling of women in public, prohibitions against the marriage of a Muslim and a non-Muslim, criminalizing pregnancy out of wedlock (even if the woman is raped), prohibitions against homosexuality (repeat offenders are subject to the death penalty), laws against criticizing or denying any part of the Quran (again, punishable by death), and (perhaps most mystifying of all) the criminality of buying, selling, or consuming alcohol. (!) And there's a bunch more: premarital sex, gambling, the eating of pork, getting a tattoo, eating pork *while* getting a tattoo (I would imagine), being outside of your home unescorted if you're a single woman—these are just some of the many laws that fundamentalist Islamic countries have implemented based on their readings of the Quran and the Hadith. Punishments include flogging, stoning, and, in the case of thievery, the amputation of hands and/or feet. (Drinking a beer will get you flogged.) These guys play hardball.

Judaic fundamentalism can be pretty rigid and uncompromising too. Fundamentalist observers of the faith insist on a strict reading of what's known as the Halakha, the collective body of Jewish law sourced in the Torah. Orthodox Jews believe the Halakha to be divine. According to this tradition, the Torah includes no less than 613 commandments by which one must live. These commandments include some fine ones, like to not stand by idly if a human life is in danger and to not bear grudges. Others include orders not to eat lobster or shrimp, not to engage in sexual relations outside of marriage, not to remain married to a woman who has been unfaithful (even if you've patched things up), not to initiate a divorce if you are a woman, not to leave the house or do any work on Shabbat (the Jewish Sabbath, observed weekly from sundown on Friday until sundown on Saturday), not to object to the execution of a false prophet, not to sell your Hebrew servant as a slave (presumably, you can sell other servants as slaves), and other commandments that might be seen by many as being, well, let us say outdated?

With Christian fundamentalism, the central tenet is the belief that unless one accepts Jesus Christ as one's Lord and savior, one is bound for Hell, described in the Bible as a "lake of fire" with much "wailing and gnashing of teeth" and the song "Achy Breaky Heart" playing on repeat *forever*.[3] Now, the concept of Hell makes a certain amount of sense from a philosophical perspective. I mean, what *does* happen to us when we die? Well, if the idea of the conscious mind being more sophisticated than mere brain matter is correct, something that perhaps the brain has given rise to, then it stands to reason that the conscious mind would survive the death of the brain. I can imagine it as just sort of floating away from the body. There's no reason to believe that consciousness would cease to exist, but it also makes sense that it would now be unable to change because the mechanism that allows for change and growth of the mind (the brain) is no longer functioning and feeding it. If

---

3. Just kidding. (It's actually "Macarena.")

this is the case, when you die, you'd more or less be the sum total of whatever your mind is. You'd lose the power to think, reason, or make choices. You'd be what you've been.

If the universe is conscious, if everything is conscious, then I can conceive of your consciousness merging with the consciousness of the universe, becoming one with it. The means of Earthly separation—the body (in particular, the brain)—no longer being a factor. If your mind is roughly in alignment with God, you'd merge with God. You'd become one with God! Like a drop of water becoming one with the ocean. But if it wasn't, if, say, you had the mind of a Hitler or a Stalin or a Jack the Ripper, then, by logic, you wouldn't be able to join God. A God that is good, which is to say loving, merciful, compassionate, and all those other eternal attributes that help define God, would be unable to abide a mind that is largely the opposite of those things. Not just unwilling, mind you, but logically unable. It would be oil and water. You'd go unrecognized by God. And that's what Hell would be, not a lake of fire but a condition of total separation forever from God and all that is good. Complete and utter aloneness. And without the ability to change.

The fundamentalists would reject this philosophical approach to Hell and swear that "lake of fire" is the accurate description because this is what it says in the Bible, and the Bible is the divine Word. There's no real reason, by the way, to make this leap about the divine nature of the Bible. Literalists typically claim it is so by referencing scriptural verses that confirm its divine nature, which is a bit like me claiming every word in the book you're now reading is true because I'm saying, *right here in this book,* that it's true. (Actually, it's not "a bit" like that; it's exactly like that.) At any rate, literalists believe in the lake of fire, which, as everyone knows, is Hell. Now, since we've all "sinned and come short of the glory of

God" (as it says in Romans), fundamentalists believe that we're all headed to the lake of fire. You, me, Heinrich Himmler, Pol Pot, Osama Bin Laden, and Joan who works down the street at the flower shop. You know Joan. Short gal? With that bob haircut? Nice as can be, Joan is. I've never heard a bad word come out of her mouth. Nevertheless, she's coming with us to the lake.

Fortunately, God has provided a solution, and that solution is Jesus. Jesus has atoned for our sins by willingly being crucified, spilling his blood for our benefit. All we need to do is believe in Jesus, ask for forgiveness, our sins will be washed away, and we'll be able to avoid the lake of fire and be welcomed, instead, to Heaven, a really, *really* nice place where they've never even heard of "Achy Breaky Heart." But you have to accept Jesus. Being good isn't good enough.

Interestingly, for all the importance of it, Jesus himself never talked that much about his death as atonement. He mentioned it at the Last Supper, but you'd think, as humankind's sole solution to the afterlife problem (a pretty big problem, you have to admit), that Jesus would have been more forceful and repetitive in telling us why he was really here. That should have been the only thing he ever talked about, and it should have been such a prominent theme of his everyday conversation that nobody would have had to guess about it years later. He should have talked about it so much that his disciples would have eventually said, "Okay, Jesus, we *get* it. For crying out loud, can you talk about something else for once?"

And this is where the atonement idea is both bad philosophy and bad theology. The problems are threefold. First, the vagueness of the atonement idea, as talked about by Jesus himself. Second, it's far from clear how, or why, the whole atonement thing works. How—exactly—does Jesus's death make the rest of us poor slobs acceptable in Heaven? How does believing in Jesus and asking for forgiveness cleanse you of sin exactly? You're still an imperfect being. You're still short of the glory of God. Well, apparently, it works because God makes the rules about this sort of stuff, and this is what he's decided on. But this makes one wonder why he couldn't have used a better approach to begin with, which brings us to the third problem, namely, the astonishing ineffectiveness of this solution.

How many people in the history of humankind have accepted Jesus as their Lord and savior and sought forgiveness? I mean, deep down in their hearts, the way you're supposed to? What percentage would you say? When you consider all the people who came before the crucifixion, all the people who have subscribed to other religions throughout time, all the people who have never heard of Jesus or understood the atonement, and all the people who merely pay lip service to the idea—I mean, let's be realistic. Has even one percent of the world's total population throughout history done what's required, according to fundamentalists, to avoid the lake of fire? It's probably a tenth of that amount. Maybe a hundredth. Maybe one in every thousand. But for the sake of argument, I'm willing to say one percent; the atonement has an effectiveness rate of one percent.

This is bad. By anyone's definition, the atonement project has to be considered an abject failure. Would you get on a plane if the chances of arriving at your destination alive and intact were one percent? Would you allow yourself to be operated on by a surgeon who loses 99 percent of his patients? What would happen to a baseball manager who lost 99 percent of his games? He would be summarily fired and rightfully so. Nobody would put up with that.[4] I can't think of a single occupation where a one-percent success rate is acceptable. (Well, maybe spam or telemarketing, but the stakes are pretty low.)

In the interest of accuracy, the oft-quoted John 3:16 verse might as well be rewritten as "For God so loved the world, he created an atonement program that has an effectiveness rate of less than one percent." All of which has to make one wonder why anybody would worship a god that performs at such a disastrous level of ineptitude. What makes such a god worthy of any respect at all? Now, fundamentalists would argue that (somehow) we're all given the chance to accept Jesus, and it's not God's fault if we blow it. But this is passing the buck. If this were the way things truly worked, it *would* be God's fault. I used to be in marketing. If a marketing campaign for a product didn't work, we didn't spend time blaming the potential customers. We didn't say, "Idiots. Can't they see, with our wonderful campaign, how good the product is? Screw 'em!" No, we *changed the campaign*. We took into account the market's fickle nature and the desires and motivations and hot buttons of the prospective customers. We conducted market research and put together focus groups. We got into the customers' heads and learned ways to speak their language. *We found what worked*. And we reached them.

Fundamentalist Christianity just doesn't make any sense. Fundamentalist Islam isn't doing much better with the oppressiveness of its Sharia law. Fundamentalist Judaism lacks modern-day relevance. I don't mean any of this disparagingly. Hey, if you're a fundamentalist and you're still reading (which I would find stunning),

---

4. In fact, in the so-called modern era of baseball, the worst record belongs to the 1916 Philadelphia Athletics, but even they won 23.5 percent of their games, going 36–117 that year.

then more power to you. You can believe what you want. And I'm aware that by defining, in part, the practice of fundamentalism as an exercise in exclusion, I risk being hoisted on my own petard. Am I excluding fundamentalism? Well, maybe. But remember that my core criticism is that fundamentalists believe they are God's chosen people. God's attention and love are drawn exclusively to them. As you may be gathering by now, or will certainly find clearer as we progress, I have no such beliefs about any particular religion or worldview.

The fact is, I think we do our great religions a disservice when we take their holy texts literally or take uncompromising views with an exclusionary approach. Stuck in the trees, we fail to see the forest and miss a point or two. Chaim Steinmetz, Senior Rabbi at Congregation Kehilath Jeshurun in New York City, puts it like this, speaking of Judaism but with words that could apply just as easily to the other Abrahamic religions: "Fundamentalism doesn't fail because it's extreme; it fails because it is soulless. While fixating on reading every word of the text correctly, it forgets to listen for the voice of God."

Chapter Fourteen

THE STUFF ABOUT GOD: ISLAMIC PANENTHEISM, JUDAIC PANENTHEISM

T he thing about fundamentalists is that they tend to get all the headlines. They make the most noise. They're the ones, after all, who go to war for their beliefs. It's the fundamentalists who preach on street corners and scream at passersby that the end is near and that repentance is required. They like to flaunt their beliefs and even politicize them. They're bores, quite frankly. There, I said it. Heck, you know what I'm talking about; you've met them. You say, "Nice day today, huh?" and they start talking about how you need to be saved or that you're never going to make it to paradise because, hey, you're eating a pork chop and drinking a glass of wine. Maybe at one time you've even been a fundamentalist. Maybe that's why you're here.

If so, then you know that these people give religion a bad name, driving more people away from God than bringing them to God. Over time, most people begin to think of a religion only by how it's presented by the ranting fundamentalists, thus providing them with only two perceived theological choices: fundamentalism or atheism. No wonder so many people choose the latter. Maybe that's why you've chosen, or are contemplating, the latter.

With Islam, for example, we hear a lot from radical Islamists, those pressing for Sharia law, and even committing terrorist acts. Lost in all of the rancor is a group of Islamic adherents known as Sufis, practitioners of *Sufism*. Sufis don't spend a lot of time concerned about the power structure of their religion or the many unyielding rules thereof. They don't waste a lot of effort engaged in trying to convert others, either, whether by gentle persuasion or by threats to life and limb. They're more interested in Islam's spiritual aspects. You know, the stuff about God.

Muhyi ad-Din Ibn al-'Arabi, henceforth shortened to Ibn 'Arabi (1165–1240 CE), was a Muslim scholar, theologian, philosopher, poet, and mystic from the region of Murcia in Spain. To say that Ibn 'Arabi was a prolific writer would be like saying that the Grand Canyon is a pretty big ditch. He is credited with 850 works and has been studied for his writings and beliefs ever since he put them down. He was perhaps more philosopher than theologian, often referred to as "Plato's son." He is known to those who practice Sufism as "The Greatest Teacher."

Unlike the fundamentalists of Islam, Ibn 'Arabi felt that there was room for all sorts of different beliefs. To Ibn 'Arabi, each way, however it might appear to be in contradiction to another, is a valid manifestation of reality. Reality, in fact, is made up of diversity and even paradox. ("Do I contradict myself?; Very well then I contradict myself; I am large, I contain multitudes.") According to Meena Sharify-Funk (Wilfrid Laurier University, Ontario)[1] and William Rory Dickson (University of Winnipeg),[2] for Ibn 'Arabi, "unity and multiplicity are different aspects of one reality. Multiplicity is not an illusion; rather, it is the result of a single reality being filtered through different points of view that are in states of perpetual transformation." And there is a unifying force

---

1. Associate Professor, Department of Religion and Culture.

2. Associate Professor of Islamic Religion and Culture.

behind the multiplicity that Ibn 'Arabi referred to as the "unity of existence," an all-encompassing principle that allows for all worldviews. Said Ibn 'Arabi, "The knower of God... accepts all kinds of beliefs, but does not remain tied to any figurative belief."

My goodness. Contrast that with fundamentalism. Note that by declaring this, Ibn 'Arabi is saying that even a fundamentalist is not wrong. Rather, the fundamentalist's beliefs are sourced in their "point of view," which has come to them "filtered," as Sharify-Funk and Dickson put it. (Literalism is an interpretation, remember.) The fundamentalist should not "remain tied to" those beliefs or to that single point of view.

Within multiplicity, "there is connection to the incomparable One, who transcends all plurality and duality." And this transcendent One can be recognized here on Earth: "His qualities can be made immanent in the world through the purified human being, who acts as a means of expressing these divine qualities."

Transcendent *and* immanent. Remind you of anything? Yes, Sufism is alive with panentheistic thinking; again, way before the word "panentheism" was even coined by Western philosophers. For Sufis, one needs to recognize both the transcendent and immanent natures of God to properly understand God (as much, that is, as God is understandable). According to Ibn 'Arabi, "If you affirm transcendence you bind. If you affirm immanence you define. If you affirm both, you hit the mark. You are an Imam in knowledge and a master."

In fact, Muslims have various names for God, each describing an attribute. The transcendent and the immanent natures are called, respectively, *al-Batin*, meaning "the hidden," and *al-Zahir*, "the apparent." All names point toward *Al-Ismul Azam*, translated as "the Greatest Name," but the real name behind *Al-Ismul Azam* is supposedly known only to prophets. For Ibn 'Arabi, all the names were aspects of God that connected potential forms with created forms. And if that reminds you of Whitehead's eternal and actual entities, it should. Ibn 'Arabi, "son of Plato," was a damn fine philosopher.

Now, God's immanence is observable aside from just "through the purified human being." According to Japanese scholar Toshi-hiko Izutsu (1914–1993), who first translated the Quran into Japanese, the Absolute is beyond the world, and yet "the Absolute has an aspect in which it appears in each creature." So there's something of God in all. And not only does the Absolute have an aspect in which it appears in each creature, but according to Ibn 'Arabi, God never manifests himself in the same way twice or to two people in the same way. Each person, at each moment, has a unique experience of reality. Or, put alternatively, God manifests himself to each person at each moment in a new and different way. Creation is forever new; God's self-manifestation is forever changing. I mean, seriously, this sounds like it came right off the pages of *Process and Reality*.

And it has profound implications. As Sharify-Funk and Dickson put it, "If God manifests himself in all things, in all beliefs, to all people, in different ways, then the true worshiper of God worships God in all of these forms."

The tragic part of all of this is that radical fundamentalists hate the Sufis for these beliefs. They are constant targets in countries like Pakistan, Somalia, Egypt, Libya, Iran, and lots of other places. Targets, that is to say, of other Muslims, fundamentalist Muslims who consider Sufi beliefs blasphemy. The Taliban hates them. So do al-Qaeda and ISIS. Bombings, killings, the destruction of holy Sufi shrines—it's a continual barrage. (If you're hated by the Taliban, al-Qaeda, and ISIS, you know you're doing something right.)

Thankfully, we're more open-minded in the West. Wait—are we? In 2009, a Sufi community center and cultural space were proposed in New York City, two blocks from the World Trade Center site of the 9/11 attacks. Nobody in the area seemed to have a problem with it, but word leaked out, and your more divisive political types jumped all over it, dubbing it the "Ground Zero Mosque." The story went national, with legendary political divider Newt Gingrich memorably declaring, "Nazis don't have the right to put up a sign next to the Holocaust Museum in Washington. We would never accept the Japanese putting up a site next to Pearl Harbor. There's no reason for us to accept a mosque next to the World Trade Center." Nobody seemed to care, or knew, that Sufism stands directly opposed to terrorist acts like what were carried out on 9/11. It didn't seem to matter that the Sufis had been targeted by the same people who targeted the United States, that the haters of the United States were also the haters of Sufism. Muslims are Muslims, and Islam is Islam. Today, the once-future home of a peaceful Sufi community center is the site of a condominium project.

With respect to Judaism, what's most interesting for our discussion is the relationship, according to Jewish texts, between God and His people. As Rabbi Bradley Shavit Artson of the American Jewish University in Los Angeles notes, God is portrayed as passionate and changing, a god even of "shifting" emotions. "God rejoices (Deuteronomy 28:63), delights, smells (Genesis 8:21), gets angry (Exodus 4:14), loves (Deuteronomy 7:17), even repents (Genesis 6:6, Exodus 32:14, 2 Samuel 24:16, Amos 7:3)." This is obviously far from the dispassionate and unmovable sky god. This is an accessible, feeling God.

Now, one can take those texts literally or metaphorically. We made mention earlier of God's engagement with people in the

Torah/Old Testament, a very active God at that. It would be logical to assume that these are symbolic stories meant to demonstrate God's capacity to be affected by the actions of human beings. A God, in Whitehead's words, that is "the great companion—the fellow sufferer who understands." Remember, it is the inability of God to act (at least directly) that helps us deal with the problem of evil.

Rabbi Artson, however, postulates another solution to that problem, paying heed to Isaiah 45:7: "I form the light, and create darkness: I make peace, and create evil: I the LORD do all these things." For Artson, pain is an "unavoidable corollary to sentience, and a greater capacity for enjoyment." His is a God "who is supremely excellent in evil, holding the suffering, and working to transform it into repentance, healing, justice, and love." Evil has a reason, in other words. It's the launching point for good.

Either way one wants to consider the matter, evil is a part of the universe, and the universe is a part of God, thus creating a not-so-tidy world. Artson asserts that "a *panentheistic* [emphasis mine] understanding of God recognizes the undomesticated nature of all reality and responds with awe and wonder." The "undomesticated nature" means unpredictability. With this understanding of the universe, Artson notes, freedom is built into the world, indeed encouraged by God's directive in Genesis to "be fruitful and increase." For Artson, this is a hidden plea for creativity, Whitehead's fundament of all.

And the universe is changed by freedom and its consequent creativity. God is changed. God is affected. God feels. Is this the God you imagined when you started reading this book?

But, of course, that's the immanent nature of God. As we know by now, with panentheism, there is a transcendent nature, too, and it turns out that there is much in the traditions of Judaism that seems to confirm this point of view. The Talmud says that God's presence is in all places. In fact, a common rabbinic term for God is *Ha-Makom*, meaning "the place." But God is more than "the place," as in our universe of spacetime. According to the Bereshit Rabbah, a midrash (commentary) on the Book of Genesis from around 500 CE, "God is the place of God's world, but God's world is not God's place." This seems as good a definition of panentheism as we are likely to find, says Artson, and I would agree. The totality of God is not in this world. God is here, but here is not the eternal, transcendent God.

Nevertheless, God's nature is revealed here, meaning that (Artson again), "Focusing our attention within the world is no longer a philosophical/logical break from contemplating the divine." We don't have to look elsewhere. We don't have to contemplate a separate "out there somewhere" God. God is here. God is more than here, but God is here. God is this place.

One particular school of Judaic thought that embraces panentheism is *Hasidic Judaism*. So does *Kabbalah Judaism*, a form of Jewish mysticism. What is *mysticism*, by the way? You hear the word all the time. In fact, earlier in this very chapter, I described Ibn 'Arabi as a "mystic." What the heck does this mean? Well, to put it simply, mysticism (which, importantly, is not exclusive to any one religion) describes a relationship with God. But not just any relationship. Mysticism refers to becoming "one" with God, or the Absolute, or the Universe, or the Eternal (or however God is described). You could say that a mystic is someone who is *really* in alignment with the divine. Or, at the least, someone who has had an experience or experiences of union with God. Again, this suggests a highly accessible God, highly accessible because God is here, now, in everything.

But being panentheistic, God is more than here. A Kabbalist believes in the spacetime God and *Ein Sof*—the eternal, mysterious God. The task of a believer is mystical union with God and the revelation of God to the world, a bit, once again, like Whitehead's idea of actual entities prehending eternal objects to become, in Kabbalist thought, something revelatory of God: a beautiful, collaborative, creative act. Note how close this is to the Sufi idea of God's qualities being made immanent in the world through the purified human being, who acts as a means of expressing these divine qualities.

The thing about this idea is that Kabbalists maintain that it has been in existence since Eden. This is no newfangled way to consider God. Far from it. Different texts have come along that confirm it, but these are believed by Kabbalists to have originated from oral traditions that started at the very beginning of human time. It's been treated as rather esoteric, however, information available only to a select few. In fact, "esotericism" is a description that scholars often use to categorize a broad range of mystic worldviews. Perhaps it's no big surprise that the word "mystic" can be traced to the Greek *mystikos*, meaning "secret" or "connected to the mysteries."

Even still, it's had its influence on mainstream religious thought. Tamar Ross (Bar-Ilan University, Israel)[3] speaks of how Judaic theology has had a tendency to adjust over time, "a restless zigzag, persistently seeking... to accurately calibrate a precise Archimedean point between the classical theistic picture and a more panentheistic model."

Maybe all of religion is like this. Maybe all of religion recalibrates as time goes by, seeking that point that best describes the truth of our world. Maybe this is part of the creative process of the universe,

---

3. Professor Emeritus of the Department of Jewish Philosophy.

a natural evolution. But not according to the fundamentalists, of course. The Islamic fundamentalists and the more orthodox Jewish faithful have no patience for such ideas. Nor do the Christian fundamentalists. But to paraphrase the Bard of Avon, Christianity, as we will see next, has—like Islam and Judaism—more to it than is dreamt of in the philosophy of the fundamentalists.

CHAPTER FIFTEEN

ABOUT THE WHOLE JESUS THING: CHRISTIAN PANENTHEISM

I n 1094, Archbishop Anselm of Canterbury (1033/3–1109) began writing what became a classic work of theology entitled *Cur Deus Homo?*, or *Why was God a Man?* In this work, Anselm (later to become Saint Anselm) first outlined his "satisfaction theory of atonement." This theory postulated that the reason Jesus was crucified was to make satisfaction for humankind's disobedience, which dishonored God. Someone needed to *atone*, you see. Humans acquired a debt to God: we've *wronged* God by sinning against him (by harming his creation and not worshipping him, among other things), and we must, in some sense, pay this debt back to God. Jesus, on the other hand, lived a perfect life—a life free of sin. And so he owed no debt to God. In light of this, he gave his life as a payment for the debt of humankind (if only we'll accept it), thereby satisfying our debt to God and making us right again with him. In other words, Jesus's death atoned for our sins. Jesus suffered for us to satisfy our debt to God, and we no longer have to die and suffer in Hell (so long as we accept Jesus's death on our behalf).

This was groundbreaking at the time because it replaced the ransom theory of atonement, which basically held that Jesus's death satisfied a ransom paid to Satan to keep us out of Hell. That had been a popular theory since the fourth century, or, roughly, three hundred years after the crucifixion. Anselm didn't especially like the idea that God would actually capitulate and pay a ransom to Satan. Couldn't God simply overpower Satan? Everyone jumped on board Anselm's theory, including, in the sixteenth century, the Protestants of the Reformation, although they had a slightly different take. French theologian John Calvin (1509–1564) believed in what would become known as "the penal substitutionary theory of atonement." Jesus's death was not to restore God's honor but to pay for our sins. It was a form of justice, and Jesus received our punishment for us.

What's interesting to note about the atonement issue is that—as British author and former Roman Catholic religious sister Karen Armstrong points out in her extensively researched *A History of God*—there were "no detailed theories about the crucifixion as an atonement" for three hundred years after Jesus's death. "Paul and the other New Testament writers never attempted a precise definitive explanation of the salvation they had experienced." And no one even seemed to talk about it, not until the fourth century. A cynic—I don't know, let's call him G. S. Payne—might note that this was at a time when Christianity was not much more than a fledgling religion: a worldview gaining traction only in fits and starts, and most certainly in need of a publicity boost, something to make it more compelling for the masses, like, say, the threat of eternal damnation offset by the promise of salvation. And the theories didn't really become honed and polished for more than a thousand years after the crucifixion until Anselm and then again 500 years after that with John Calvin. Again, one is prompted to wonder why Jesus himself didn't spend more time on this most critical issue, *the* most critical issue, since it involves *everybody's* eternal life. Why is there a need for theories at all? (And—no small

point—there have been at least seven major theories of atonement.) During the Sermon on the Mount, Jesus had the attention
of "multitudes," according to Matthew. Couldn't he have used
the opportunity to nail this thing shut? In almost 1200 words, he
never once mentioned anything about his mission of atonement.
Doesn't this seem odd? He talked of Hell, but the way out of it
was obedience, not atonement.

In his book, *The Universal Christ*, prominent Franciscan priest
Richard Rohr (b. 1943) calls Anselm's *Cur Deus Homo?* "unfortunately" the most successful piece of theology ever written. Its
legacy was "disastrous." Rohr, perhaps unsurprisingly, prefers the
less-publicized Franciscan viewpoint. The Franciscans, a religious
order founded by Francis of Assisi (1181–1226), "claimed that the
cross was a *freely chosen revelation of Total Love* on God's part." It
was not a source of payment to God for a debt owed by humans.
It was something much more than that.

And therein lies the potential beauty of the Christian religion.
If we take ourselves away from fundamentalist doctrine for a moment, what might we uncover? Rohr, as it happens, is a panentheist. And it turns out that if you pair Christianity with panentheism, you open the door to a whole new view of Jesus. Jesus,
presented as God incarnate, becomes a conduit between the transcendent God and the immanent God. Whitehead's dipolar God
becomes one in Jesus, providing us with the prototypical example
of alignment with God. I mean, that's pretty cool. It's Sufism's
purified human being. According to Rohr, "Jesus was meant to be
the guarantee that divinity can indeed reside within humanity." He
quotes Athanasius of Alexandria (c. 296–298 – 373), who wrote,
"God became the bearer of flesh so that humanity could become
the bearer of Spirit forever." (Why did people back in the year 300
know more than we do?)

For Rohr, Jesus was the second incarnation. The first was Genesis, when God became the universe. Or, more precisely, "when God joined in unity with the physical universe and became the light inside of everything." Or, as recorded in John 1:3, "All things came into being, and not one thing had its being except through him." God in all. The second incarnation—God becoming man—was in the form of Jesus Christ, but Rohr differentiates between "Jesus" and "Christ." The former was God in human form; the latter was God: "Christ is God, and Jesus is the Christ's historical manifestation in time."

For New Testament scholar and theologian Marcus Borg (1942–2015), this difference between "Jesus" and "Christ" is apparent if you compare and contrast the synoptic gospels with John. Matthew, Mark, and Luke—all written before John—detail the historical Jesus, reading almost like news accounts. John, as we've discussed, is written more like a theological treatise. Borg, in *Meeting Jesus Again for the First Time*, notes that the contrast is such that "both cannot be accurate characterizations of Jesus as a historical figure." John's characterization is clearly different, speaking of something more than "Jesus" the man, a portrait, Borg says, that is "essentially one of the Christ of faith, and not the Jesus of history. [In the synoptic gospels,] Jesus never spoke of himself as the Son of God, as one with God, as the light of the world, as the way, the truth, and the life, and so forth. Indeed, he never spoke the words of John 3:16." Now, to be completely accurate, there are indeed references in the synoptic gospels to the theological meaning of Jesus's life (even if Jesus himself does not articulate them), but the difference in emphasis between the synoptics and John is unmistakable. And John takes on a completely new vibe if you read it as though he is writing of Christ—*God*—and not Jesus.

Or, as Borg puts it, "the post-Easter Jesus," which he defines as "the living Christ of Christian experience."

This is the Christ we can all experience, the Christ-*ness* that Jesus experienced in spades as God's human manifestation. Panentheism allows for this because with panentheism, everything is, to some degree, a manifestation of God, with the degree predicated, perhaps, upon the level of alignment. Jesus might have been *really* in alignment. "The core message of the Incarnation of God in Jesus," says Rohr, "is that the Divine Presence is here, in us and in all of creation, and not only 'over there' in some far-off realm." Jesus is called the "light of the world" in John, but in Matthew, he asserts (to the multitudes in the Sermon on the Mount) that "*Ye* are the light of the world." See that? We're all the light of the world. God—Christ—is in us. The Apostle Paul, in his letter to the Galatians, speaks of "the Son *in* me." In his second letter to the Corinthians, he declares that a true test of faith is whether or not you've acknowledged that "Jesus Christ is in you." In Colossians: "Christ is all and in all." Rohr points out that Paul uses the phrase "*en Cristo*" (in Christ) "more than any single phrase in all of his letters: a total of 164 times."

Jesus himself speaks of the divinity in all when he says in Matthew, "Verily, I say unto you, inasmuch as ye have done it unto one of the least of these my brethren, ye have done it unto me." God is even in the least of us!

Remember those ancient texts found in the Egyptian town of Nag Hammadi in 1945? Literalists call them apocryphal, but listen to this verse from the text known as the Gospel of Truth: "The gospel of truth is a joy for those who have received from the Father of truth the grace of knowing him.... For he discovered them in himself, and they discovered him in themselves." This was the position of the *Gnostics*, second-century Christians who believed that gnosis—the knowledge of spiritual mysteries—could be found within because the Christ was within. In her important bestseller *The Gnostic Gospels*, Elaine Pagels writes, "Realizing the essential Self, the divine within, the gnostic laughed in joy at being released from external constraints to celebrate his identification with the divine being." The divine as internal, not external.

One can consider Jesus as a human in great alignment with the universe (a purified human being) or as a symbol of God as human, but either way, the New Testament is full of important things Jesus had to say that have nothing to do with atonement. Like about love, for instance. Or, as I pointed out earlier, the eloquent and relevant-to-this-day Sermon on the Mount. In that sermon, Jesus said, among many other wise things, "Do not worry, saying, 'What shall we eat?' or 'What shall we drink?' or 'What shall we wear?'... Do not worry about tomorrow, for tomorrow will worry about itself. Each day has enough trouble of its own." This is good stuff. Now, philosopher and endlessly entertaining writer-speaker Alan Watts (1915–1973)[1] noted that most people react to this by saying something like, "'That's all very well because Jesus was the boss's son and he knew that he had nothing to worry about, but we have to be practical.' Well what do you suppose the Gospel was? It was the *good news*.... You too are the boss's son: that was the gospel." Jesus is telling us that we're *all* in God, and that everything is going to be A-OK.

Interestingly, Eastern Orthodox Christianity seems to grasp this panentheistic view of Christianity more so than the Western brands of Christianity, painting things in a much more positive and loving light than the God-fearing fundamentalists. Literally. In *Resurrecting Easter*, scholar and historian John Dominic

---

1. I recommend reading anything by Alan Watts.

Crossan (b. 1934) and his wife Sarah write of the difference in art and iconography between Eastern and Western Christianity, noting that images created in Western Christianity depict the resurrection of Jesus as a solitary, individual affair, with Jesus "rising in splendid, triumphant, and transcendent majesty, but also in splendid, triumphant, and transcendent isolation." Eastern art, on the other hand, portrays Jesus rising, but as he does so, "he reaches out toward Adam and Eve, the biblical parents and symbols for humanity itself, raises them up, and leads them out of Hades, the prison of death." He raises *all* of humanity *with him*, you see.

The artwork is important because, as the Crossans note, there is no description in the Bible of the actual Resurrection, of Christ's emergence from the tomb. This is interesting in and of itself. There are descriptions of every other part of Jesus's ministry (even colorful descriptions of his birth that we've made Christmas carols out of) but not of this critical piece of Christian theology. And so we are left to rely on the artists, and isn't it fascinating the way East and West differ in this regard? The Crossans refer to the Western tradition as the "individual resurrection tradition," a tradition unfortunately consistent with the idea that each individual is eternally screwed unless he or she accepts the Western idea of Jesus as his or her "Lord and savior." The Crossans refer to the Eastern tradition as the "universal resurrection tradition." We're all a part of God. Christ is here for all of us. I think I like the Eastern tradition better.

Russian philosopher Nicolas Berdyaev (1874–1948) had this to say about the East–West divide: "The central idea of the Eastern Fathers was that of *theosis*, the divinization of all creatures, the transfiguration of the world... not the idea of personal salvation." This was not only the central idea of the Eastern faithful but the main initial idea of all the faithful. "Only later," Berdyaev tells us,

"Christian consciousness began to value the idea of hell more than the idea of the transfiguration and divinization of the world." The main message got lost. "The Kingdom of God is the transfiguration of the world, the universal resurrection, a new heaven and a new earth."

What else have mainstream Western Christians missed? Well, the feminine essence of God for one thing, hence the patriarchal nature of the religion. Does it really make sense that God would be male? A fatherly or grandfatherly figure? A bearded, masculine judge? If all is in God, then God is both male and female, and that makes a hell of a lot more sense if you ask me. Now, it must be said that there's no church doctrine, per se, that stipulates God's gender, but certainly God's maleness has been implied, and the lack of the feminine nature of God is hard to deny. Everyone says "He" or "Him" or "Father," and that has an effect on general perception, whether intended or not.

Interestingly, in Paul's letter to the Galatians 3:28–29, he writes, "There is neither Jew nor Greek, there is neither slave nor free, there is neither male nor female; for you are all one in Christ Jesus." This seems to reflect Genesis 1:26–27, which tells us that God said, "Let us make man in our image, after our likeness... in the image of God created he him; male and female created he them." God's image seems to be both male and female. How did this idea get so lost?

And there has been a ton of symbolism that has generally been neglected. Rohr posits that the Eucharist or Holy Communion—the ritual commemoration of the Last Supper, where the faithful are given bread and wine and told, as Jesus told his disciples, that the bread is Jesus's body and the wine his blood—is a reminder of God in all. Says Rohr, "Eucharist is the Incarnation of Christ taken to its final shape and end—the very elements of the earth itself." Put in a more poetic way, "We are not just humans having a God experience. The Eucharist tells us that, in some mysterious way, we are God having a human experience!"

There is, of course, much symbolism in the crucifixion and resurrection. Christ's suffering on the cross is a reminder that God suffers with us. God feels what we feel, remember? According to Rohr, "A crucified God is the dramatic symbol of *the one suffering* that God fully enters into *with us*—much more than just *for us*, as we were mostly trained to think." Whitehead's fellow sufferer who understands.

For the Crossans, having studied the artwork of Eastern Christianity, well, religiously, the resurrection is a symbol of deliverance for all humankind. "When Christ, rising from the dead... grasps the hands of Adam and Eve, he creates a parable of possibility and a metaphor of hope for all of humanity's redemption."

Some scholars believe the resurrection, the prototypical symbol of flesh becoming spirit, is an example of sacrificing what's often referred to as the "ego" self for the "true" self, putting our selfish desires away for something bigger, something more in line with the desires of the universe for each of us. It's about getting in alignment! If this is the case, perhaps no words in the New Testament are more important than the words that were, according to Luke, spoken by Jesus in the Garden of Gethsemane as he contemplated his impending death: "Not my will, but thine be done." Maybe this should be the prayer for all of us. If you're hellbent on subscribing to an atonement theory, this one might be a good candidate. After all, think of the word itself: *at-one-ment*. "Atonement" at one time specifically meant to become *at one* with. This is the etymology of the word. To reconcile; to be in harmony with.

Or perhaps the resurrection is simply a reassurance that life does not end upon death. Now, none of this is to state categorically that the resurrection didn't happen. Maybe it did. Think about this: there were a lot of guys who ran around in the time of Jesus saying they were the next messiah, some of them amassing big followings. The historian Josephus recorded a dozen or more. Typically, sooner or later, these messiahs would cross a line, and the government would have them put to death. In time, Jesus obviously became the most popular, but we all know who the second most popular was, right? Of course not. Nobody remembers any of these guys. They were executed, their followers buggered off, and we never heard anything more about them.

Something different happened with Jesus. The followers stuck around. And then their numbers grew and continued to grow. Some of them were even put to death for their beliefs, but the movement never stopped. This is pretty remarkable. This Jesus fellow must have been pretty impressive, and for all we know, maybe he did appear to some of his followers after his death. At the least, maybe they had visions of him of some kind. This is what Marcus Borg believed, postulating that Jesus's followers "continued to experience Jesus as a living reality after his death. In the early Christian community, these experiences included visions or apparitions of Jesus." Religious experiences! Just like we discussed earlier. Such is the impression Jesus made that he was still experienced after his death. Maybe even today?

The book of John is all about this experience, which is why it reads so differently from the synoptic gospels. Writes Borg, "Why would the early Christian community out of which John's gospel comes portray Jesus as saying about himself, 'I am the light of the world,' 'I am the bread of life,' 'I am the way, the truth, and the life,' if Jesus did not speak that way about himself?" For Borg, it's because that's how they "experienced the post-Easter Jesus." Christ, not the historical man. And hence, the beauty of John, if read in the right light.

Now, were these religious experiences visions, apparitions, dreams? Maybe Jesus was literally resurrected. For Borg, it didn't really matter. The resurrection works just fine as metaphor. With the resurrection story, Jesus overcame the power structure of the time. The government put him to death, but there's a much larger power, one beyond Earthly powers. For Borg, the resurrection's central meaning "is both religious and political: the lords of this world crucified Jesus, but Jesus is Lord, and they aren't." In fact, the disciples talk about seeing not the historical Jesus after his death but "the risen Lord." Moreover, there are powers we all have to face. There are problems we all have to overcome. According to Borg, "Death and resurrection become a metaphor for the internal spiritual process that lies at the heart of the Christian path."

It speaks of a transformative process, in other words. Paul says this in Galatians when he claims, "I am crucified with Christ." He didn't mean it literally, obviously. He's speaking in metaphor. "Nevertheless I live," he continues, "yet not I, but Christ liveth in me." Ego self to true self. Jesus even hinted at the metaphor himself while he was still alive, saying in Matthew, "Whosoever will come after me, let him deny himself, and *take up his cross* [emphasis mine], and follow me." Writes Borg, "Good Friday and Easter embody the path that Jesus taught: the path of dying to an old way of being and being born into a new way of being."

What's interesting about this viewpoint is how much the focal point of Christianity changes from the fundamentalist perspective. Borg speaks of the historical Jesus as "a spirit person, one of those figures in human history with an experiential awareness of the reality of God," further defining him "as not simply a person who believed strongly in God, but one who knew God." For Borg, this image "shifts the focus of the Christian life from believing in Jesus or believing in God to being in relationship to the same Spirit that Jesus knew."

This is huge. Christianity isn't really about Jesus. Or even believing in Jesus. And it isn't about "being saved" from the lake of fire. It's about one's relationship with God, a relationship accessible to all. To know "the Spirit that Jesus knew." And to be transformed by this relationship, to experience the divine *within*. This was the message of Jesus, and that explains why he didn't waste a lot of words on the atonement idea. Or, to sum it up in the words of Thomas Aquinas, the saint from the thirteenth century who, as you'll recall, gave us the cosmological argument for God's existence: "The Son of God became human in order that humans might become gods."

Chapter Sixteen

Ninety Days from Now

W hy did we just spend so much time on religion? This is a book about the existence and nature of God. Isn't a discussion on religion beyond our scope? Maybe even beside the point? I don't think so. Can you see, in the threads of the Eastern religions, in Sufism, in Kabbalah Judaism, in a non-fundamentalist view of Jesus Christ—can you see in all of these long-established yet less-well-known worldviews the God that I have proposed in this book?

Panentheism, far from being some obscure, unrecognized philosophy, is in actuality a metaphysic that goes back thousands of years and has presented itself in myriad ways through *every major religion* on the planet. We're not inventing anything here. We're shining a light on a perspective that has been known since the dawn of humanity. The major religions have been embracing a panentheistic worldview all along. But maybe you're familiar with these great religions only through their noisiest branches, the fundamentalist factions. If so, it's possible that you might have missed some pretty important stuff.

Earlier, I conceded that the texts of these religions cannot prove God, but I wondered if maybe God could prove the texts. Hopefully, you can see what that means now. The texts of every religion are powerful when you regard them as reflections of the divine. Perhaps the people who claim that texts like the Old and New Testament were divinely inspired are right on the money, at least inasmuch as the people who wrote them were in alignment with the divine: God was writing through them, or maybe more accurately, they were writing through God. Knowing that God exists and understanding something of God's nature, we may find that the texts take on a different, more significant, and even more beautiful meaning.

Okay, so with all of that said, where are we now? We've covered a lot of ground together, and you've been a terrific audience. You followed along as I presented the Big Ten arguments *for* God's existence (with some better than others); tried my best to refute the Big Six arguments *against* God's existence; proposed first one conception of the universe (pantheism) and then another (panentheism); took that second conception and measured it against our arguments for and against God; addressed in particular the thorny problem of evil; and then connected this conception of the universe (God) with all the major religions, arguing against the more strident, darker fundamentalist perspectives before introducing you to the more rational, exalted, and uplifting perspectives.

At the beginning of this book, I proposed a standard: that it's more reasonable to believe in God than to not believe. I also conceded that nobody can define "reasonable" in this particular case but you. Only you can say whether the arguments herein render it more reasonable than not to believe in God's existence.

So, what do you say?

Has the standard been met? What if you had to put a percentage on it? Are you 90 percent sure now? 75 percent? 51 percent? I'll take 51 percent; 51 percent meets the standard. For that matter, so does 50.000001 percent.

I hope you're at least 50 percent sure.[1] If not, might I ask why? Maybe I can guess. It's hard, isn't it? It's hard to change one's worldview. Hell, it's hard to change one's haircut. I don't know about you, but I have a difficult enough time adjusting to the clock changes every spring and fall. Changing one's worldview? The way one considers the very nature of reality? Yeah, that might be even harder. Especially since it's so much easier to just stay the course.

Changing anything about one's life means, first of all, overcoming inertia. So, if you're still unsure, if you're under 50 percent (and yet still interested), allow me to offer a simple, risk-free, *gradual* approach to belief in God. Here's what you do: for the next ninety days, go about your life like normal, except for one slight adjustment. Pretend there's a God. Let's call this *Payne's wager*. You don't have to believe there is a God, mind you; you just have to pretend. For three months, pretend this world was brought into existence by a supremely creative force and that this force exists in everything. Pretend there's an underlying intelligence to the universe. When you see a sunset or a painting that moves you, imagine that the beauty you recognize is a gift from that intelligence. When you share a special moment with a loved one, imagine that you are not merely reacting to chemical processes in your brain but that you are tapping into something beyond both of you. Think of your conscious mind, and try to conceive of a larger, universal consciousness that it's a part of. Imagine for a little while that you are not alone in the cosmos. Imagine that there's a fellow traveler with you, a fellow sufferer who understands you, who understands your moments of joy and sorrow. Who feels what you feel. And who can give you rest, guidance, and hope.

And love.

---

1. For one thing, you'd owe me a beer. (Wasn't that the bet?)

Talk to this traveler. Talk to God. You don't have to do so in any kind of formal, prayerful way, and I sure wouldn't expect you to do it in front of anybody. But in a moment of solitude, introduce yourself. If you're stuck, you could do a lot worse than heed the suggestion of Proverbs 2:3 and "call out for insight and cry aloud for understanding." But you don't have to call and cry; just ask. Ask for insight and understanding; see if you can tap into the wisdom that's here for you, the wisdom that's always been here.

After ninety days of this, see if the world doesn't start to seem just a little more magical, a little more welcoming, a little more special. See if your life feels richer, deeper, more connected.

See if you feel less alone.

It's a cheap bet. You're betting ninety days of your life, and if nothing happens, so what? At least you tried, right? Atheism will wait ninety days. It's not going anywhere. You have the rest of your life to be an atheist. You can at least give three months to this little experiment.

In a sense, I am asking you now to embrace Pascal's wager and/or the existential argument for God's existence. Remember those? Pascal said that we have nothing to lose by believing and much to gain. The existential argument is essentially a pragmatic one. If believing gives you hope and comfort, then why the heck not believe? Saint Augustine said, "Unless you believe, you will not understand." Faith precedes reason. If you're still on the fence, if you're still a doubter, if you're still a skeptic, but you're at least curious, then Payne's wager might be a way to decide, through the experience of believing, whether believing is for you. Think of it like a test drive.

But maybe there's another reason for your resistance besides simple inertia. Maybe you're afraid of what it will mean to become a theist. Might that be it? You're going to have to start going to church every Sunday. You're going to have to start memorizing and quoting scripture and trying to convert your friends. You're going to have to start saying, "God be praised!" whenever something good happens, clapping your hands together and looking to the sky. You're going to have to start wishing strangers a "blessed" day. Drinking, smoking, swearing—all things of the past. Movies with violence and adult situations? Not for you anymore. You're going to have to be *religious* now.

In the immortal words of the legendary Sergeant Hulka: "Lighten up, Francis." *None* of these things has to happen. You can maintain your current lifestyle.[2] And you can keep your newfound spirituality (if that's what it is) entirely to yourself, if you want. You can keep it a secret! At least for now. Maybe later, you can decide to share it with others, but you don't have to try to convert anybody else, and you don't have to bark scripture at people. For most of my life, I have kept my spirituality close to my vest. I have friends and relatives who will be surprised to read this book, in fact. I consider my relationship with the universe to be between me and my God. I don't mind talking about it or, obviously, writing about it, but to me, it's a very personal thing. Your thoughts about God are nobody's business but yours.

Now, if you decide at some point that you want to share those thoughts, then do so. Maybe you'll even decide to celebrate those thoughts with others. Maybe you'll decide to join a religion of like-minded people. For what is religion? Religion, at its best, is a way to experience, through ritual and tradition, one's relationship with the universe (God). Christians celebrate Easter every year to remember the resurrection, and you might want to celebrate with

---

2. Unless of course you're a serial killer or some other kind of active criminal. Then you probably ought to stop.

them to remind yourself of the transformative process of finding the divine within, the ego self sacrificed for the true self. Jews celebrate Passover, commemorating the escape of the Israelites from bondage in Egypt, at least in part as a reminder to escape the feeling and control of our egoistic, divisive world and to enter the feeling and control of the higher, altruistic, united world. Muslims, especially Sufis, engage in a form of meditation called *dhikr*, in which prayers and aphorisms are chanted repetitively as a way to develop and practice awareness of the divine that is always present and to recognize God as being here and now. Hindus do something very similar with a practice called *japa*.

Every religion has its traditions and rituals. And they're all ways to engage *in the same thing*: bringing oneself closer to God. To connect, in other words, with the underlying intelligence of the universe. To put oneself in alignment.

But for what purpose? That's a fair question, and a big one. Maybe you're now 51 percent sure that God exists. So what? If you were 51 percent sure that it was going to rain this afternoon, you might still proceed with your picnic plans, right? In other words, what difference does it make if you come to believe in God? What changes? What *is* the natural evolution of a spiritual life?

Here, I believe we are led back to Alfred North Whitehead to remind us of our creative natures. We are partners in the ongoing creativity of the universe, each of us with a means by which to participate, to make something, to change the world by our presence. It is our purpose to give the underlying intelligence of the universe form and meaning. We paint, we write, we heal, we manage, we build, we buy, we sell, we care, we love. We are. Martin Luther King, Jr., once said, "If a man is called to be a street sweeper, he should sweep streets even as Michelangelo painted, or Beethoven composed music, or Shakespeare wrote poetry. He should sweep streets so well that all the hosts of Heaven and Earth will pause to say, 'Here lived a great street sweeper who did his job well.'"

Is there a larger purpose beyond even that? Maybe. But I don't happen to think so. It's creativity for the sake of creativity. People wonder what the meaning of life is. You might as well ask, What's the meaning of a rose? It *is*. That's the meaning. Being in alignment means finding and following your particular creative purpose, and there's no more meaning than that, nor does there ever need to be. And the purpose might change. It might even change from day to day. But if you're true to yourself—your true self, that part of you that is connected to the divine—you'll follow where that purpose leads. God will participate in the universe through you.

And you'll never be alone.

The purpose of a spiritual life is not to get into Heaven. That will happen anyway because nothing is lost in a universe of consciousness. God, says Whitehead, "saves the world as it passes into the immediacy of his own life. It is the judgment of a tenderness which loses nothing that can be saved." In a world that's conscious, your consciousness will always find a home. Rather, a spiritual life is about the here and now, the eternal now because there *is* nothing else. Now is time*less*, and this is what eternal means, not everlasting. This is what Jesus meant in the (non-canonical) Gospel of Thomas when he said, "The Kingdom of the Father is spread out upon the earth, and men do not see it."

Ah, but these are all things for you to discover. I have said enough. You might find other truths. But how will you know if you reject the concept of God? And as for religion itself, if you decide to seek fellowship with like-minded people to experience through ritual and tradition a greater relationship with the divine, I wouldn't dare recommend one religion over another. If you've gathered nothing else from my words in this book, you should have gathered that. I will tell you honestly that I am a Christian. I was raised Presbyterian. I'm familiar with the traditions. I love the story of Jesus, and the symbology outlined in the last chapter is glorious to me. Did Jesus do everything it says he did in the Bible? Does it matter? As a friend of mine once said, "Point me to whoever wrote the Sermon on the Mount, and I will follow him."

Conceptually, I think Christianity is beautiful. I engage in the rituals, and they've become meaningful to me. Every Christmas Eve, I attend a candlelight service, and I never fail to get a lump in my throat when the congregation sings "Silent Night," just as the congregations of years past sang it, just as the congregation of my parents sang it, and that of my grandparents, and my great-grandparents, and all the people who have come before me and took part in this tradition. The church is filled with nothing but candlelight and radiant music, and every year, I'm reminded of the song "Walking in Memphis" and Marc Cohn's musical answer to the question, "Tell me, are you a Christian, child?": *Ma'am, I am tonight*. How could I not be?

But I have studied Buddhism, too, a religion that I appreciate for the simple fact that it is more philosophy than dogma. Everybody knows to appreciate the present moment, to slow down and smell the roses, right? But we never do. Buddhists have made a religion out of this. Buddhism puts things in perspective like no other way of thinking. The Buddhist concept of suffering as a result of erroneous attachment to the fleeting stuff of the world is impossible to deny. Their concept of the no-self is likewise. We take ourselves too seriously. Buddhism recognizes this. Buddhism also recognizes the absurdity of life. Had Albert Camus chosen a religion, I believe it might have been Buddhism. And this recognition means that we're all fellow travelers trying to make sense of this wonderfully strange thing we call life, and this is why Buddhism places so much emphasis on compassion. Christianity emphasizes love. I'm not ashamed to admit that I struggle with this. I can't bring myself to love complete strangers, let alone enemies, as advised by Jesus. I can have compassion, though. I can imagine that the guy who cut me off in traffic and then flipped me the bird this morning was having a bad day and maybe even a bad life. I can have compassion for him. But do I have to love him? I don't know.

Compassion, of course, is not foreign to Christianity, and indeed, some believe this is exactly what Jesus was getting at when he admonished us to love our enemies. He meant for us to consider the world from their perspective, to move beyond ourselves and around to their side to try to see what they see. This engenders compassion, perhaps the one common denominator of all theologies. As Karen Armstrong put it in her beautiful memoir *The Spiral Staircase*, "Compassion was the litmus test for the prophets of Israel, for the rabbis of the Talmud, for Jesus, for Paul, and for Mohammed, not to mention Confucius, Lao-tzu, the Buddha, or the sages of the Upanishads."

I guess if I had to describe my religion, I'd say I'm a Panentheist Christian Absurdist Buddhist. I'm a P-CAB. See? You can be anything you want to be. It's up to you. Maybe you want to study firsthand some of the religions we've discussed in this book. Maybe you want to talk to practitioners. Perhaps you want to dive deeper into the sacred texts of the major religions. Or maybe you want to order some unbiased educational books and read further about different religions in general, or about God, or about philosophy. Maybe you want to check the ideas of the book you are holding against books that have countering ideas. That's fine, too. In fact, I would encourage it. You don't have to take my word on any of this.

My hope is that this book might be the start of something for you, whether it's the start of a spiritual journey or the start of further research generated by the stirrings of curiosity. But I'm aware that it can never be more than that: a start. The next steps belong to you and only to you. No two journeys are ever the same. Remember what Ibn 'Arabi said: God never manifests himself (herself?) in the same way twice or to two people in the same way. Each person, at each moment, has a unique experience of reality.

So don't ever listen to anyone who speaks in absolutes, and yes, I heard the contradiction, and I don't care. The point is that you are a creative instrument of the universe, and you need to find your own beautifully unique way to proceed. I would only say in closing, and as a final word of encouragement, that those who seek God often come to discover something pretty cool, and that is this: while they were seeking God, God, all along, was seeking them.

ACKNOWLEDGMENTS

I thanked them in the introduction, but I need to thank them again here. Dr. Loriliai Biernacki of the University of Colorado, Dr. Matthew Benton of Seattle Pacific University, and Dr. Perry Hendricks of the University of Minnesota, Morris. I don't know which was more valuable – your careful review, or your enthusiastic encouragement. Both were needed. A million thanks.

Endless gratitude is owed to each and every one of my ghostwriting clients. I can't think of a better, more gratifying, more humbling way to have honed my skills than by helping you tell your amazing stories. God bless you all.

Michael Schur, you don't know me but your *How to Be Perfect* provided the model: philosophy can be fun, even entertaining. I owe you a beer. Maybe two.

Glossary

Absolute idealism: Everything is mind, and physicality is an illusion. See also *panpsychism*.

Actual entities or occasions: A. N. Whitehead's terms for things made manifest in the universe by God. See also *eternal objects*.

Aesthetic argument for God: There is the music of Mozart; therefore, there is a God.

Argument from divine hiddenness: If God exists, why doesn't he reveal himself?

Argument of incompatible properties: God cannot exist due to certain logical paradoxes, such as God's alleged involvement in space and time even though God created space and time and must, therefore, be external to them.

Atonement theories: Theories developed many centuries after the execution of Jesus Christ to explain how Jesus's death reconciled God and humans.

Canonical gospels: The officially sanctioned accounts of the life of Jesus Christ: the books of Matthew, Mark, Luke, and John found in the New Testament.

Glossary

Contradictions-of-religion argument: AKA *the argument of inconsistent revelations* or *the avoiding-the-wrong-Hell problem*. Essentially, if God exists, why are there so many conceptions and scriptures, many of which are in opposition to each other?

Cosmological argument for God: Something (i.e., the universe) cannot come out of nothing; hence, there must have been a prime mover, i.e., God. Or, the assertion that time must have had a starting point.

Creativity: A. N. Whitehead's ultimate metaphysical principle underlying everything, even God.

Empiricism: Belief that all knowledge is ultimately grounded in sense experience (including scientific experiments) rather than reason.

Epistemology: Study of knowledge. What do we know, and how do we know we know it?

Eternal: That which is beyond/not of our universe. See also *immanence*.

Eternal objects: A. N. Whitehead's terms for potentialities, entities in the abstract. See also *actual entities or occasions*.

Existential argument for God: It's useful or beneficial to believe in God, so God exists.

Forms: Plato's concept of eternal, unchanging entities. See also *universal*.

Fundamentalism: Belief in a worldview that excludes all other worldviews and considers them false. See also *literalism*.

Gnostics: Second-century Christians who believed that (among other things) knowledge of spiritual mysteries can be found within because the Christ is within.

God of the gaps: Term used to describe the presumed fallacy of explaining the seemingly inexplicable by invoking the concept of God.

Hard (or causal) determinism: Belief that every occurrence, including every action, is the necessary result of all that has come before, leaving no room for free will.

Hasidic Judaism: Jewish religious group that recognizes God as immanent.

Historical record argument for God: The argument that holy texts prove the existence of God.

Immanence: Here and now. See also *eternal.*

Justified true belief: The not-infallible theory that something can be considered knowledge if one is justified in believing it to be true.

Kabbalah Judaism: A religious school of thought that considers the relationship between the mysterious, eternal God and the immanent God.

Literalism: Interpretation of holy texts as being true in their most literal sense. See also *fundamentalism.*

Mind–body dualism: Belief that the mind and body are two distinct substances.

Moral argument for God: Morality exists; therefore, a standard of morality must exist; therefore, God exists.

Glossary

Mysticism: Belief in the idea of experiential union with God.

Non-propositional knowledge: Knowledge of something typically gained through experience and/or direct awareness. See also *propositional knowledge*.

Occam's razor: Named after medieval philosopher William of Occam, the theory that when considering two competing ideas, it's generally a good idea to pick the one with fewer assumptions.

Ontological argument for God: If God can be conceived of as the greatest of all beings, then God must exist because the greatest of all beings *would* exist; otherwise, it would not be the greatest of all beings.

Panentheism: "All in God." Belief in a fixed, eternal, transcendent God and an immanent, right-here, right-now God. See also *pantheism*.

Panpsychism: Belief that although objects might be physical, they are imbued with mentality, even consciousness. (Compare with *absolute idealism*.)

Pantheism: "All is God." Belief that everything is God. See also *panentheism*.

Pascal's wager: If you choose to believe in God, you have everything to win and very little to lose. If you choose not to believe in God, you have everything to lose and very little to win. So you should choose to believe in God.

Payne's wager: A bet wherein the wagerer lives with the idea that God exists for a three-month period to see if the idea resonates.

Pornography theory of truth: Like Supreme Court justice Potter Stewart with respect to porn: you can't define truth, but you know it when you see it.

Pragmatism: School of thought that considers knowledge and truth by their usefulness and practical application.

Prehending, prehension: A. N. Whitehead's term for how minds perceive information from actual occasions and eternal objects that have been made manifest in the universe so as to create new things. See also *actual entities or occasions* and *eternal objects*.

Prevalence-of-religious-experience argument: God must exist because so many people claim to have experienced something of God.

Principle of limitation/determination/concretion: A. N. Whitehead's terms for God.

Problem of altruism: Monkey wrench in the theory of evolution. What explains self-sacrifice?

Problem of evil: Argument against the existence of a good God on the grounds that evil exists.

Propositional knowledge: Knowledge that something is true, either by empirical or rational means. See also *justified true belief*.

Rationalism: Knowledge by argument or line of reasoning.

Snake handling: Definitive proof that it takes all kinds to make a world.

Skepticism: Belief that nothing can be known, not even whether anything can be known.

Glossary

Sufism: Islamic body of mystic religious practice.

Synoptic gospels: From the Latin *synopsis*, meaning "a seeing altogether," used to refer to the very similar gospels of Matthew, Mark, and Luke.

Teleological argument (or intelligent design): God exists as surely as a watchmaker must exist to make a watch.

Temporality: In time or related to time.

Theological noncognitivism argument: God cannot exist because the very concept of God makes no sense.

Transcendence: Beyond, as in beyond the mind, beyond the physical, or beyond the universe of space–time.

Universal: Eternal, unchanging mode of something. See also *forms*.

Notes

Chapter 1

4. A recent Pew Research poll: Many Americans Mix Multiple Faiths, Pew Forum on Religion & Public Life, Pew Research Center, Dec. 2009.

6. Another Pew Research report: Masci, D., *Scientists and Belief*, Pew Research Center, 5 Nov. 2009.

12. Bertrand Russell: Russell, B., *Human Knowledge: Its Scope and Its Limits*, George Allen & Unwin, 1948.

12. In 1925, Moore wrote a famous essay: Published in *Contemporary British Philosophy* (2nd series), ed. J. H. Muirhead, 1925 Reprinted in G. E. Moore, *Philosophical Papers* (1959).

Chapter 2

19. Bertrand Russell once put it like this: Russell, B., *A History of Western Philosophy*, Simon and Schuster, 1947, p. 568.

23. This passage is from Hawking's landmark book: Hawking, S. *A Brief History of Time*, Bantam, 1988, p. 136.

25. For instance, physicist and professor Paul Davies: Davies, P., *The Accidental Universe*, Cambridge University Press, 1982, p. 89

25. In fact, as philosopher and author Jeffrey Koperski: Koperski, J., *The Physics of Theism*, Wiley-Blackwell, 2015.

26. British mathematician and astronomer Sir Fred Hoyle: "Hoyle on evolution," *Nature*, Vol. 294, No. 5837, 12 Nov., 1981, p. 105.

26. American biologist Edwin Conklin: *Edwin Grant Conklin Papers*, 1897–1952, Princeton University Library.

29. In his book The Scientific Companion: Emiliani, C, *The Scientific Companion*, John Wiley and Sons, 1988, p. 149.

Chapter 3

35. In fact, theologian Graham Stanton: Stanton, G., *The Gospels and Jesus* (2nd ed.), Oxford University Press, 2002, p. 145.

38. It starts out as something like: The Godfather, Paramount Pictures, Dir. Francis Ford Coppola, 1972.

38. For instance, as Hebrew scholar Millar Burrows: Burrows, M., *The Dead Sea Scrolls*, Moody Press, 1986, p. 304.

Chapter 4

40. And so if nature doesn't provide it: Lewis, C. S., *Mere Christianity*, Geoffrey Bles, 1952.

Notes

43. *If I had let that young man go*: "Sacrifice and Bliss," *Joseph Campell and the Power of Myth*, episode 4, PBS, 1988.

45. *John Stuart Mill (1806–1873), a prominent ethicist*: Mill, J.S., "Theism" in *Three Essays on Religion*, Henry Holt & Co., 1874

46. *French Enlightenment philosopher Voltaire*: Voltaire, "Remarks on Pascal's Thoughts," 1728.

48. *In fact, Ludwig Wittgenstein*: Rhees, R., Ludwig Wittgenstein: *Personal Recollections*, Rowman & Littlefield, 1981, p. 105. (The remark was reported by Wittgenstein's student Maurice O'Connor Drury.)

Chapter 5

51. *The Pew survey mentioned above*: *Many Americans Mix Multiple Faiths*, Pew Forum on Religion & Public Life, Pew Research Center, Dec. 2009.

51. *German philosopher Friedrich Schleiermacher*: Schleiermacher, F. quoted in *Brief Outline for the Study of Theology*, tr. William Farrer, 1850.

52. *Another German thinker*: Otto, Rudolf, *The Idea of the Holy*, Oxford University Press, 1923.

52. *This book, taken from a series of lectures*: James, W. *The Varieties of Religious Experience: A Study in Human Nature*, Longmans, Green & Co., 1902.

55. *David Chalmers (b. 1966)*: Chalmers, D., "Facing Up to the Problem of Consciousness," *Journal of Consciousness Studies*, 2(3):200-19, 1995.

57. *Interesting aside: back in 1998*: Horgan, J., "A 25-Year-Old Bet about Consciousness Has Finally Been Settled," *Scientific American*, 26 Jun. 2023.

57: *Apparently, she was left speechless*: Cairns-Smith, A. G., *Evolving the Mind: On the Nature of Matter and the Origin of Consciousness*, Cambridge University Press, 1996, p. 197.

60. *In his book* The Existence of God: McCabe, J., *The Existence of God*, Watts and Co., 1918, p. 84.

62. *But this rose is an extra*: Doyle, A.C., "The Adventure of the Naval Treaty," *Strand Magazine*, Oct.-Nov., 1893.

Chapter 6

65. *There's a famous thought experiment*: Introduced by Hilbert in a 1924 lecture "Über das Unendliche," reprinted by Ewald, W., Sieg, W. in *David Hilbert's Lectures on the Foundations of Arithmetics and Logic 1917-1933*, Heidelberg: Springer-Verlag, 2013.

68. *Gerald Joyce, chief science officer*: Robertson, M. P., & Joyce, G. F., "The Origins of the RNA World," *Cold Spring Harbor Laboratory Press*, 2012.

68. *Harold Bernhardt, Research Fellow:* Bernhardt, H. S., "The RNA world hypothesis: the worst theory of the early evolution of life (except for all the others)a," *Biology Direct* 7, 23 (2012).
69. *And if that's true, then there must be consciousness:* Chalmers, D. *The Conscious Mind,* Oxford University Press, 1996.

Chapter 7
74. *God is "infinitely grander:* Drummond, H., *The Ascent of Man,* 1904, p. 333.
75. *"We may define the essence of a unicorn,":* Smith, G. H., *Atheism, the Case Against God,* Prometheus Books, 1979, p. 64.
77. *Saint Anselm of Canterbury:* Anselm, *Proslogion.*
78. *Although people have been asking questions:* Schellenberg, J., *Divine Hiddenness and Human Reason,* Cornell University Press, 1993.
80. *It knows nothing of beautiful and ugly:* From Erwin Schrödinger's lectures, "Nature and the Greeks" and "Science and Humanism."
80. *And that is because, in the last analysis,:* Planck, M., *Where is Science Going?* George Allen and Unwin Ltd., 1933, p. 217.
80. *"Over the entrance to the gates:* Planck, 214.
81. *"And from within me:* Wiesel, E., *Night,* Hill and Wang, 1960, p. 65.
81: *The tragedy of the believer:* Wiesel, E., "The Tragedy of the Believer," interviewed by Krista Tippett, *On Being,* 20 Nov. 2003.
84. *There are, in fact, some 4,200 religions:* "World Religions Religion Statistics Geography Church Statistics." Archived from the original 22 Apr., 1999.
84. *Historian–philosopher and atheist Stephen F. Roberts :* Posted by Roberts on the alt.atheism newsgroup, 1995.
85. *I didn't, either:* https://www.gordonconwell.edu/center-for-global-christianity/research/quick-facts/.
85. *But what if God's essence:* Whitman, W., "Song of Myself" from *Leaves of Grass,* Norton, 1973.
88. *You may attribute miracles to Him:* Lewis, C.S., *The Problem of Pain,* The Centenary Press, 1940.

Chapter 8
95. *It wasn't until 1697:* Raphson, J. *De Spatio Reali,* 1697.
96. *Here's what he said:* Singer, D.W., *Giordano Bruno: His Life and Thought,* Henry Schuman, 1950, p. 179.
98. *Thoreau felt he was born:* Thoreau, H., "The Pond in Winter.," essay from *Walden; or, Life in the Woods,* 1854.
98. *"We followers of Spinoza,":* From a letter to Eduard Büsching, Oct. 25, 1929, *Einstein Archive,* reel 33–275.

Notes

Chapter 9
100. *'It is only to enrich our language:* Schopenhauer, A., *Parega and Parlipomena,* 1851. Retrieved Oct., 2023, Cambridge University Press.

100. *Richard Dawkins put it:* Dawkins, R., *The God Delusion,* Black Swan, 2007., p 99.

102. *And as influential as* Principia Mathematica *was:* Whitehead, A. N., *Process and Reality,* The Free Press, 1985, (Original work published 1929.)

107. *John B. Cobb, Jr. (b. 1925):* Cobb, J., *A Christian Natural Theology: Based on the Thought of Alfred North Whitehead,* Westminster Press, 1965.

Chapter 10
109. *Well, as John Cobb, Jr. has pointed out:* Cobb Jr., J. B., *Whitehead Word Book: A Glossary with Alphabetical Index to Technical Terms in Process and Reality,* P&F Press, 2008, p.23.

113. *Our man William James:* Perry, R., *Thought and Character of William James,* Little, Brown and Co., 1935, p. 446. (Perry references James's Harvard lecture notes from 1905-06)

113. *A recent gathering of physicists and philosophers:* Falk, D., "Is Consciousness Part of the Fabric of the Universe?" *Scientific American,* 25 Sept. 2023.

Chapter 11
121. *Schopenhauer put it like this:* Schopenhauer, A., "On the Freedom of the Will," essay presented to the Royal Norwegian Society of Sciences 1839, tr. Konstantin Kolenda, Bobbs-Merrill, 1960.

125. *Alfred North Whitehead could be complicated:* Whitehead, A. N., *Process and Reality,* The Free Press, 1985, p. 346. (Original work published 1929.)

126. *The human body, like every other:* Kaneda, T., & Haub, C., "How Many People Have Ever Lived on Earth," *PRB,* 15 Nov. 2022.

128. *"God," Whitehead wrote:* Whitehead, p. 351.

129. *And then he concluded:* Camus, A., *The Myth of Sisyphus,* Tr. Justin O'Brien, Hamish Hamilton, 1955, p. 152. (Original work published 1942.)

129. *He talks about it in his book:* Lewis, C.S., *A Grief Observed,* Faber and Faber, 1961.

129. *He talks about it in his book: Shadowlands,* Warner Brothers, Dir. Richard Attenborough, 1994.

Notes

Chapter 12

130. Either way, the Purusha: Purusha Sukta, Rig Veda, 10.90.3-4, in F. Max Muller, ed., *Rig-Veda-Sanhita: The Sacred Hymns of the Brāhmans together with the Commentary of Sayanacharya*, 2nd ed., vol. IV, Oxford University Press Warehouse, 1892, 288–289.

131. In fact, according to Loriliai Biernacki: Biernacki, L. Clayton, P., *Panentheism across the World's Traditions*, Oxford University Press, 2013.

131. "I bow to him who pierces: Abhinavagupta, *Īśvara Pratyabhijñā Vivṛti Vimarśinī* [IPVV], p. 255.

132. According to the Ācārāṅga Sūtra: Herman Jacobi, trans., *Jaina Sutras, Part One* (Oxford: Clarendon, 1884), 19, I:2:4.

132. "This definition of soul: Chapple, C.K., "Life All Around: Soul in Jainism," *Panentheism across the World's Traditions*, Oxford University Press, 2013, p. 102.

133. "Each individual actual entity,: Whitehead, p. 56.

133. For the Jain religion: Chapple, p. 104.

134. "[It's] what underlies: Lee, Hyo-Dong, "The Heart-Mind of the Way and the Human Heart-Mind are Nondual: A Reflection on Neo-Confucian Panentheism," *Panentheism across the World's Traditions*, Oxford University Press, 2013, p. 39.

134. Pattern is the metaphysical ultimate: Lee, p. 40.

134. It is "the ultimate structure or 'logic': Lee, p. 41

135. As Samuel puts it,: Samuel, G., "Panentheism and the Longevity Practices of Tibetan Buddhism," *Panentheism across the World's Traditions*, Oxford University Press, 2013, p. 87.

136. *(Whitehead said this idea:* Whitehead, p. 342.

Chapter 13

137. Christianity is the first,: Hackett, C., et al., "The Future of World Religions: Population Growth Projections, 2010–2050," Pew Research Center, 2 Apr. 2015.

140. It's why Shakespeare wrote: Shakespeare, W., *Romeo and Juliet*, Act 2, Scene 2.

140. Or why Tom Cochrane wrote: Cochrane, Tom, "Life is a Highway," Capitol Records, 1991.

147. Chaim Steinmetz, Senior Rabbi: Steinmetz, C., "Where Fundamentalism Fails," *Jewish Journal*, 26 Aug. 2022.

Chapter 14

149. Multiplicity is not an illusion: Sharify-Funk, M; Dickson, W.R., "Traces of Panentheism in Islam: Ibn al-'Arabi and the Kaleidoscope of Being," *Panentheism across the World's Traditions*, Oxford Univ. Press, 2013, p. 146.

Notes

150. *Within multiplicity*: Sharify-Funk, Dickson, p. 148.
150. *And this transcendent One*: Sharify-Funk, Dickson, p. 149.
150. *According to Ibn 'Arabi*: Sells, M. A. 1994. *Mystical Languages of Unsaying*, University of Chicago Press, 1994, p.100.
151. *According to Japanese scholar Toshihiko Izutsu*: Izutsu, T., *Sufism and Taoism: A Comparative Study of Key Philosophical Concepts*, University of California. 1983. P. 52.
151. *Creation is forever new,*: Sharify-Funk, M; Dickson, p. 154.
151. *As Sharify-Funk and Dickson put it*: Sharify-Funk, M; Dickson, p. 155.
152. *The story went national*: Interview on "Fox and Friends," Fox News, Aug. 9, 2010.
152. *"God rejoices:* Artson, B.S., "Holy, Holy, Holy! Jewish Affirmations of Panentheism," *Panentheism across the World's Traditions*, p. 22.
153. *For Artson, pain is:* Artson, p. 24.
153. *Artson asserts that:* Artson, p. 25.
154. *According to the Bereshit Rabbah:* Bereshit Rabbah, 68:9
154. *This seems as good a definition:* Artson, p. 24.
154. *Nevertheless, God's nature is revealed here:* Artson, p. 30.
155. *Tamar Ross (Bar-Ilan University, Israel) speaks of how:* Ross, T., *Traditional Concepts of God and Kabbalistic Interpretation: An Overview*, TheTorah.com, 2014.

Chapter 15

158. *What's interesting to note about the atonement issue*: Armstrong, K., *A History of God: The 4,000-Year Quest of Judaism, Christianity, and Islam*, Ballentine Books, 1993, p. 87.
159. *In his book,* The Universal Christ: Rohr, R., *The Universal Christ*, Crown Publishing, 2019, p. 142.
159. *The Franciscans, a religious order:* Rohr, p. 143.
159. *According to Rohr,:* Rohr, p. 178.
159. *He quotes Athanasius of Alexandria:* Athanasius, "On the Incarnation 8," trans. Oliver Clement, *The Roots of Christian Mysticism*, New City Press, 1995, p. 263.
160. *For Rohr, Jesus was the second incarnation:* Rohr, p. 12.
160. *The former was God in human form:* Rohr, p. 19.
160. *Borg, in* Meeting Jesus Again for the First Time,: Borg, M. J., *Meeting Jesus Again for the First Time*, HarperCollins, 1994, p. 11.
160. *Indeed, he never spoke:* Borg, p. 11.
161. *Or, as Borg puts it,:* Borg, P. 49.
161. *"The core message of the Incarnation:* Rohr, p. 29.
161. *Rohr points out that Paul:* Rohr, p. 43.

162. In her important bestseller The Gnostic Gospels: Pagels, E., *The Gnostic Gospels,* Random House Publishing Group, 1979, p. 180.

162. It was the good news…. *You too are the boss's son:* Watts, A., *The Tao of Philosophy,* Tuttle Publishing, 1995, p. 48.

162. In Resurrecting Easter, *scholar and historian John Dominic Crossan:* Crossan, J. D., & Crossan, S., *Resurrecting Easter,* HarperCollins, 1989, p. 3.

163. Eastern art, on the other hand: Crossan, Crossan, p. 3.

163. The Crossans refer to the Eastern tradition: Crossan, Crossan, p. 3.

163. Russian philosopher Nicolas Berdyaev: Berdyaev, N., "Salvation and Creativity: Two Understandings of Christianity," *Western Spirituality: Historical Roots, Ecumenical Roots,* ed. Matthew Fox Bear & Company, 1981, p. 129

163. "Only later," Berdyaev tells us: Berdyaev, p. 129.

164. Says Rohr, "Eucharist is the Incarnation: Rohr, p. 138.

165. The Eucharist tells us that: Rohr, p. 137.

165. According to Rohr, "A crucified God: Rohr, P. 162.

165. "When Christ, rising from the dead: Crossan, Crossan, p. 186.

165. "Atonement" at one time specifically meant: Thurow, Joshua C., "Atonement," *The Stanford Encyclopedia of Philosophy* (Summer 2023 Edition), Edward N. Zalta & Uri Nodelman (eds.).

166. In the early Christian community: Borg, p. 13.

166. For Borg, it's because that's how they: Borg, p. 49.

167. For Borg, the resurrection's central meaning: Borg, p. 17.

167. According to Borg, "Death and resurrection: Borg, p. 19.

167. Writes Borg, "Good Friday and Easter embody: Borg, p. 19.

167. Borg speaks of the historical Jesus: Borg, p. 75.

168. For Borg, this image "shifts the focus: Borg, p. 77.

168. Aquinas, T., *Compendium Theologia,* ca. 1273.

Chapter 16

174. Jews celebrate Passover: Laitman, M., "The Meaning of Passover," The Bnei Baruch Kabbalah Education & Research Institute.

174. He should sweep streets so well: King, M.L., speech, Barratt Junior High School, Philadelphia, PA., 26 Oct., 1967.

175. It is the judgment of a tenderness which loses nothing: Whitehead, p. 346.

175. This is what Jesus meant: Gospel of Thomas, Saying 113.

177. As Karen Armstrong put it in her beautiful memoir: Armstrong, K., *The Spiral Staircase: My Climb out of Darkness,* Anchor, 2004, p. 293.

Index

Index

Index

Index

Index

Index

G.S. Payne is an award-winning ghostwriter of over forty books. In his spare time, he has always found himself drawn to "the big questions" of life, and philosophy is his major avocation. *So Who is God, Anyway: an (Un)orthodox Theory for Doubters, Skeptics, and Recovering Fundamentalists*, is the culmination of more than 30 years of philosophical research into the questions of God's existence and God's nature.

Payne lives on the Gulf Coast of Florida and when he's not writing or mulling the big questions, he can be found on his sailboat, *Pilar*, named after Ernest Hemingway's fishing boat. He also enjoys the cinema and traveling, and when engaged in the latter, he seeks out historic hotels (preferably haunted ones) and good Irish pubs. Of all the things he's most proud of, being a father and grandfather top the list

Connect with G.S. Payne at https://SoWhoIsGodAnyway.com/.

www.ingramcontent.com/pod-product-compliance
Lightning Source LLC
Chambersburg PA
CBHW050855150626
46549CB00013B/1900